DADS MAKE A DIFFERENCE
ADOPTION JOYS
BOOK 2

DORIS HOWE

Copyright © 2022 by Doris Howe

ISBN: 978-1-998784-60-8 (Paperback)

All rights reserved. No part of this publication may be reproduced, distributed, or transmitted in any form or by any means, including photocopying, recording, or other electronic or mechanical methods, without the prior written permission of the publisher, except in the case brief quotations embodied in critical reviews and other noncommercial uses permitted by copyright law.

The views expressed in this book are solely those of the author and do not necessarily reflect the views of the publisher, and the publisher hereby disclaims any responsibility for them.

BookSide Press
877-741-8091
www.booksidepress.com
orders@booksidepress.com

Contents

The Assignment Getting Ready 1
They All Got Into It 6
Two-Parent Home Benefits 7
Togetherness 9
Hispanic Mix 11
Parenting Partnership 14
A Modern-Day Pied Piper 15
No Longer Orphans 19
Children Tell Their Stories 22
A Loving Alternative 23
Bonding Experiences With My Dad 25
Security Vs. Rejection 26
Mom's Stories 29
Two Parents Give Positive Examples To Follow 30
Togetherness 31
A Strong Dad Makes 34
Strong Kids/Adults 34
Dads Plus Daughters Equals Beauty 37
Surprise! Twin Baby Girls 41
Mom Is Half The Team 43
Dad Brings Coherency 44
Service Is This Family's Middle Name 47
Adopted By The Community 49
It's All About Faith 51
Exploring Summer 53
Heavenly Father Helps Dad 56
Love Because Of And In Spite Of Differences 57
Dad's Words 59
Unexpected Life Lessons 60

Role Model For Parenting..63
An Only Child 65
Parenting Starts At Birth, But Never Ends 68
A Hands-On Dad...69
Secure With Dad And Mom 71
As The Kids Grow, The Parents Grow..73
Being Dad Is A Privilege 76
We Accentuate The Positive...78

THE ASSIGNMENT GETTING READY

God is concerned about fatherlessness that it is sweeping the culture in this country. Weekly confirmations come to my attention that a change is on the heart of God. Recently, information from a behavior workshop from the National Fatherhood Institute offers a 24-7 workshop containing twelve key behaviors centered on helping dads become all that title is in God's original plan.

The organization/ministry Promise Keepers is being resurrected also.

The book *What a Son Needs from His Dad* by Michael O'Donnell drew my attention in the Christian bookstore recently. It is another "sign" that this issue is on God's heart.

A few years ago, the Kendrick brothers made a movie called *Courageous*. Randy Alcorn wrote a novel based on the movie by the same name. The movie and the book show how a small group of men sharpened their role as Dad after some very traumatic experiences in their lives that showed them where they were deficient as dads. I highly recommend that movie as well as the book.

The numbers of unplanned pregnancies indicate that abstinence has not taken over. Yet adoptions as a choice are down. Many of the young women in this situation grew up without a dad's love and influence. She hasn't known the benefits of a dad in her life. She may feel her situation is normal. She therefore doesn't see a need to provide a dad for her child.

Some men reside in the home, but are really absent emotionally and spiritually. The *dad* influence isn't present. God's definition of family is a mom and a dad who are in partnership. They are there physically, emotionally, spiritually, and lovingly.

Webster's Dictionary defines an orphan as a child without parents.

However, a deeper look in *Strong's Concordance* goes back to the original Hebrew and/or Greek meaning of the word *orphan*. There, an orphan is defined as a child without a father. This is an explanation for the passion God has concerning the fatherlessness sweeping this country.

God gave me this assignment to put together a book of true stories that tell of the positives that have happened in children's lives because they had a mom *and* a dad. The assignment from God is solely for the purpose of emphasizing positive results for children who have had both a mom and a dad in their growing-up years. The book is not to shame anyone who didn't have a set of two parents or is a single mom through no fault of her own. It is just to tell situations that were done God's way. It is not to say that everything in these families was always positive without negatives. However, when they began to write the positives, they learned that the positives far outweighed the negatives. They were encouraged. I know these stories will be an encouragement to you as well.

Research shows that there are many benefits for a child if he/she has a father figure present in his/her life. Affectionate and supportive fathers greatly affect a child's social and cognitive behavior for the better. Children tend to have a higher self-esteem, learn better, and are less prone to depression or anxiety if they have an active father in their home and lives. Kids who grow up with an engaged father are less likely to drop out of school or end up in jail. Children growing up without a father are more likely to act aggressively or have deviant behavior. If a young child has no dad in the family, he/she may always wonder, "Am I pleasing to Mommy?" He/She may wonder why there is no dad for them to be pleasing to. That child will grow up emotionally warped if he does not have the security and assurance of his parents' love and acceptance.

I've seen loved adopted children be secure in their father's love. They are able to say no to all kinds of temptations. This is because that vacuum in their lives is already filled. They don't have to do things to win the approval of their friends when they have found absolutely security, identity, and approval in their parents' love for them and, most of all, in their heavenly Father's love for them.

This book is an assignment that God has given me. It is His passion to bring this culture back to His original plan. He has also put His passion in my spirit. Our culture has been headed to fatherlessness over the last several years. God wants His original family plan to be involved in His original design for families with purpose and passion.

When God first gave the assignment to me, I felt like Moses. "God, you've chosen the wrong person." Then I realized God does not call the "qualified." He "qualifies the called." With the Holy Spirit's constant help and the help of several families with moms and dads, I've developed the passion to carry on.

Where have all the dads gone? Is this a question that you've wanted to ask recently? This book seeks to show where some of the very successful dads are. They are a part of very successful families who have stepped forward to adopt a child or children. The stories here are true. We've changed some names to promote privacy. The mom's job is to nurture the children. She's pretty good at that. However, a child needs more than nurturing. Those children need what only a dad can bring. He is the priest in the home, the provider, the protector, and often the playmate. It is not in the female's temperament to do the jobs of a dad. Guess what. The child suffers.

Way back in the book of Genesis, God created a family. Remember it started with a dad and a mom. Even then, God said, "It is not good for man to be alone." That can also be stated, "It is not good for woman to be alone." He made the two for each other. He said, "Two are better than one. If one falls, the other can help him up."

Years ago, a popular song said, "It takes two to tango." That title's connection to a biblical statement was probably unknown to the writer of the song. Today it is as true as it ever was.

My dad was so good. He made it easier for me to embrace my Heavenly Father because of the example my earthly dad was. As I began collecting information for this book, I was reminded of the things my dad did to help me develop into womanhood. He taught me how to drink out of a Coke bottle. He taught me a strong work ethic. He taught me to shoot a gun, how to milk a cow, how to prepare a horse to ride and ride him, how to weed a garden. As young teens, our dad took my sisters and me to the basketball and football games our school teams performed. We didn't need a boy to accompany us to these sports events. We had a smart dad. After we graduated from high school, Dad said, "I can't send all three of you to college, but it's there for you. You can work your way through that higher education." My older sister and I each got two college degrees. Our younger sister worked her way through beauty cosmetology school.

After I was married and away from the home, I would visit Dad at the farm on occasion. Dad knew I was on my way. He'd hear my car approaching the farm as the car sped going up and down the hills on the country road. Dad would go out to the gate in front of the home. He'd wait there in expectation of our arrival. When we did arrive at the gate, he'd be waiting. His arms were outstretched to welcome us with a huge hug of love and welcome.

My mother was one of ten siblings. Before my dad came into that family, one of my mom's brothers died of rocky mountain fever. My grandmother never recovered from the grief of losing that child. I never saw my grandmother laugh. When our son died from a hit-and-run drunk driver, my dad was so saddened. I think he was afraid I'd not get over Joey's death as his mother-in-law didn't get over the death of one of her sons. Two days after Joey's death, my dad died. I know he died of a broken heart for me. That's positive love.

As you read this book, you'll find stories that tell of the positive experiences that happened because the dad was in the home and family. Some have just listed the events that the dads did to grow the kids into positive, secure young citizens. Each is confirmation that God's original plan for a dad and a mom is still God's desire. God doesn't change. He is the same yesterday, today, and forever.

Not every home with a man and a woman is as positive as the stories in this book. If the man is not a hands-on dad but just a provider, chances are the children won't have such good positive stories to tell. I've had the privilege of being an adoption caseworker for twenty-four years. The children depicted here have had the benefits of being placed for adoption into solid families. A single mom will choose adoption out of love for her baby. She knows she wants more for her child than she is able to provide at this time in her life.

THEY ALL GOT INTO IT

A longtime ministry, Focus on the Family, has strengthened families for over sixty years. Families who take their positions seriously have been more successful in building that family because they have learned successful families don't just happen. It takes intentionality, partnership, and unconditional love. Both mom and dad endeavor to learn successfully both jobs. The mom basically supports the dad. The dad loves his wife as Christ loves the church. He is not above changing a diaper or cleaning up spit. Each takes seriously that parenting requires participation by both.

A dad models for his sons the pattern of a godly man, husband, and dad. For his daughters, he models character qualities she will look for when she meets potential suitors in years to come.

Mom, Dad, and children are a successful unit when each gives of self to the others. Each member in these families have contributed to the beautiful whole. You'll notice that the foundations were definitely built on the *rock* of Jesus Christ.

TWO-PARENT HOME BENEFITS

In these years that I have worked with Loving Alternative Adoption Agency, I have seen God bring "beauty from ashes" over and over. We always get detailed information from the birth mom to send along with the child to his or her new life. We ask information about their personalities as well as their gifts and talents.

Over nineteen years ago, a baby was placed into a nonmusical family. This family knew the birth family was very talented in music. These new parents started exposing their baby to music from the very beginning. They played Christian music and videos round the clock. When that baby was eight or nine months old, the parents were sitting at the dinner table rehashing their day. Suddenly, they both stopped talking and listened. What they heard was a tune, on key, from that baby in the high chair at that dinner table. They recognized the melody. It was a favorite they had heard for days from a CD or a video.

When Rachel was nearly two years old, we asked her parents if they were ready to add another child to their family. The dad said, "We have so many ways we want to bless Rachel. If we adopted even just one more child, we'd need to divide what we have between Rachel and her sibling. This might mean we wouldn't be able to bless Rachel with all we dream for her." Rachel has been blessed, as you can tell from her words as well as the words of her parents. She is not spoiled. She is merely loved and blessed.

As Rachel grew to five or six years old, her parents exposed her to piano lessons for three years. Like most children, practicing wasn't her favorite activity. However, her parents persevered.

When Rachel was in middle school, she became very interested in violin. The guitar became another favorite that she loved. She was extremely talented in both instruments.

Recently she began to teach herself to play the piano by ear. She plays for hours, blessing the home and family with beautiful, relaxing piano music. Because her parents knew of the music ability in the birth family, they used that knowledge to expose their daughter to music from several sources. She has become a musical genius.

TOGETHERNESS

God has been involved in each family as they grew it in numbers. This family is no exception.

They added a new baby to their family every two years until they had four children. The journey would have been more than challenging if either the mom or the dad had to have done the parenting without the other. The following are some of the good these four kids experienced growing up because they had a mom and a dad who were in total partnership.

Dad worked the swing shift. When he came home, he'd take the midnight feeding so mom could go to bed. Then the mom could take the first morning feeding, assuring her of at least five hours of uninterrupted sleep. This then allowed the dad to sleep in and get the rest he needed for him to be ready for his "day job."

This couple learned that the first two or even three years in a child's life comes with unsettled digestive systems and/or sniffles. These situations were routinely in the middle of the night.

These needs gave the couple again the opportunities to work as a team. One could care for the child while the other teammate could clean up the sick mess. This often led to having to clean the bed as well. When the child was comforted and ready to continue the night peacefully, the clean bed helped the child relax and go back to sleep.

Early on, Dad taught the kids how to drink through a straw when they were still in a high chair. He'd capture water in the straw with his finger and let the kids suck it out. On a more pleasant note, Dad built the kids a tree house. He put up a swing set in the backyard. Dad taught the kids basic lawn mower care and how to mow and edge. Dad took care of the property so it was always safe and clean for the kids to play in the yard.

There were times that Dad pitched a tent in the backyard for "camping" adventures. He helped the kids to learn to ride their bikes. Dad took the kids fishing and taught them the details of that adventure. That built in the kids another interest in wildlife.

Because Mom and Dad were in partnership in their parenting, either Mom or Dad could do for the kids whatever they needed. This made it possible for Mom to get away from home now and then for coffee with friends, or a lunch date, or simply to get her hair done.

When the family took long car trips to visit family, the whole adventure was easier. The two parents took turns with the driving as well as with the child care.

Mom was able to stay home full-time and to homeschool because Dad supported the family financially. Both Mom and Dad have servant hearts, so the kids saw both walk with God through all the situations that come up in the lives of a family with four children. The kids saw their parents serve through their church. Their generosity was evident as they tithed and supported missions. The kids are now generous because of the parents' example.

Their first child is now twenty-two. He stated that growing up with both a mom and dad in his life has confirmed to him that adoption is a good thing. The experience solidified in his heart that he wants to adopt children of his own one day.

All together, this family is a great picture of what can happen when families walk with God through the ups and downs they encounter.

The six of them are a team as well as a family in every sense of the word. They are there for each other. Each can always count on one another to have his back. Togetherness is a label that is stamped on all the members of this family. They could be the "billboard" representing family.

HISPANIC MIX

After over a decade of trying to get pregnant, I finally got the word from the Lord that adoption was the route for me and my husband to take. I was almost thirty-nine, my husband was thirty-five, and his two children (my stepchildren) were twelve and sixteen. I had been given Loving Alternative's name and number twice throughout this infertility journey, so it was always in my mind that this was the agency for us to pursue. We attended their March orientation, returned home, and immediately made our scrapbook to give interested birth mothers a little glimpse into the window of our lives.

Around October, we were contacted by Doris and Carol that a young seventeen-year-old had requested to meet us. She was white, and the birth father was a Hispanic eighteen-year-old. God had already placed a desire in our heart for a Hispanic child, so we were thrilled… and the baby was a boy! We met with the birth mother and established a rapport and an agreement that we would adopt her son. We still talk about that beloved December day that we received that call to pick our precious gift up at the maternity home. I checked my stepchildren out of school, and the four of us headed east to get the new member of our family, who was just three days old.

Clayton's birth mother literally handed him over to me. Our emotions were all over the place, and then Carol prayed a prayer that I will never forget. She asked God for Clayton "to change nations." I saw the impact of that prayer in his life from an early age, and it is continuing today.

From day one, our family has been very open with Clayton about being adopted. As an infant and toddler, we told him he was adopted and was our special gift from God. We personally didn't want there to be a big "aha" day when he was older or when he learned about it. We just addressed questions and presented information to him as he matured through the years. That seemed to have worked well for him.

Clayton's heart grew sensitive to things of the Lord around four years old, and he accepted Jesus as His Savior when he was five. The years that followed were filled with God maturing a physically strong and independent-minded young man who has accomplished some mighty things. The "Change Nations" prayer started happening even as a toddler. Clayton donated some of his toys to victims of Hurricane Katrina, and as a preteen and teen, I've known him to give away shoes, clothes, and food at school when he knew someone was going without. His heart breaks for homeless animals and homeless people. He carried a mattress from downstairs and got his dad, me, and two dogs secured in our bathroom when an F4 tornado destroyed our home and property. As a sixteen-year-old, Clayton witnessed a bad car wreck and saved a man from the wreckage.

As a nineteen-year-old, Clayton asked me, "Mom, if you could have given birth to me or adopt me, which one would you have picked?"

I said, "Clayton, that's an interesting question, but I have to say, I would choose adoption because there have been so many blessings that have come out of this whole experience."

David has said many times that although he has two biological children from his first marriage, he has the same love for Clayton. He said that he loves Clayton with the same heart and same fatherly love. Our family is honored that God selected us to have experienced adoption and that we received Clayton from the Lord to make our family complete.

Clayton's birth mother told us that she knew she couldn't properly take care of Clayton and that she wanted him to have a dad in his life. She explained that Clayton's birth father chose to not be involved. Our family loves his birth mother, and we pray for her to have a great life. Our prayer is that deep down in her soul, she knows that she did a great thing for this child and for so many others who have known Clayton. We pray that the Lord continues to give her a peace about Clayton. He is our love and still brings us so much joy and completeness.

Clayton is appreciative of her decision to place him in our home and has commented numerous times that he wants to have his own biological children, but believes that he may adopt a child as well. With that comment, I know that he is at peace with his birth mother's decision to place him.

Clayton is an ambassador for adoption who proudly talks about who he is, where he came from, and what God has done for him. No shame ever! No guilt ever! God is merciful, and He redeems and brings glory and honor to himself. I've always told Clayton that Jesus is adopted. "He was adopted by Joseph, and if it's good enough for Jesus, it's good enough for you too!"

David said, "Being an adoptive father has been such a blessing! I cannot imagine a world without Clayton as my son. He has brought so much joy into my life. It's the best thing I have ever done. The Lord has blessed us with an awesome family! I love you, Clayton!" Love, Dad.

Clayton wrote, "Being adopted has completely changed my aspect of life. It's something that hasn't hurt me, belittled me, or isn't something that's held against me. It's something that I take great pride in, and I honestly wouldn't change that part of me for anything. I don't feel like I'm an outcast or have emotional problems dealing with my adoption that you occasionally see in movies. I'm completely blessed that God decided to put me in the amazing family he did. I have the utmost respect for my birth mother for making the right decision and placing me in great hands and changing my life for the better. Due to my personal experience with adoption, I've considered heavily on adopting in the future. Adoption is a beautiful thing, and I definitely want to play a part in an adopted child's life."

Clayton continues, "Adoption involves a triangle—the baby or adoptee, the birth mom, and the adoptive parents. Today, I'm the adoptee. It'd be a blessing for me to be part of a different adoption triangle in a different way. This time I'd be the adoptive dad. My experience is so positive. I know to be a part of another triangle in future years would be awesome."

PARENTING PARTNERSHIP

The question about why a dad is important in a family is answered with the truths stated here.

Dad works full-time to provide for the family's needs. This allows Mom to always be home with the girls.

When Mom was gone overnight on women's retreats with the church women, Dad and the girls often camped in the backyard. These outings became adventures.

Dad taught the girls to fish, to tie their shoes, how to ride a bike, how to drive a car. Dad teaching the girls about God was a lifestyle—just part of daily living.

When Mom comforts the sick child, Dad is there to clean up the vomit. When the girls were afraid for whatever reason—small or large—Dad's loving presence comforted them.

Dad helps with math homework, and Mom helps with French. Neither parent is qualified to help with the other subject!

What a blessing and a secure bonding experience as Dad saw the delight in their eyes as they went to the daddy-daughter dance, all dressed up with their date, Dad. These were learning experiences that taught them about how a lady should be treated.

Two parents in their lives brought security. Life always brings unexpected situations. During these times, both parents were able to share in all decisions, bringing joy along with the struggles that come with the responsibilities of raising children. The partnership in agreement makes the parenting more of a blessing to all in the family. Mom and Dad think differently on a lot of occasions. Mom helps them see all the options. Dad helps them see the "good" option.

This partnership is evidence that it takes a mom and a dad to make a positive difference in the lives of children.

A MODERN-DAY PIED PIPER

My husband and I have had the privilege of being parents to five beautiful children. Four of our five children happen to be adopted. Our oldest son turned twenty years old in April this year. He was our first child, and he was also adopted. The miracle of adoption is a miracle first in that the birth mom chooses life for her child, carried him to term, and was willing to give her baby a life she couldn't give at that time in her life. She wanted a two-parent home that would love and cherish her baby at least as much as she does. The second miracle is that the birth mom was willing to trust complete strangers (in most cases) to love and raise her baby better than she is able to at that time in her life.

We have had the honor and privilege to walk that out with two of our birth moms. We recently met our daughter's birth mom for the second time. The first time was right after she gave birth to our daughter. Now that our daughter is fifteen years old, we met up with her birth mom again along with her two other daughters. It was a beautiful reunion. Our twenty-year-old son met his birth mom when he was fifteen also. We felt like our children had a lot of questions that we couldn't answer. It was a very good thing for both of them. They had a lot of questions that they needed to hear the answers from their mother's mouths that brought healing. Neither one of them has regretted being adopted. They are glad that we are their parents. They have stated that we supply them a loving home and family. We have truly been blessed as a family in that our children have adopted us back and made us their family. We admit we are not perfect, but we've all grown close in the midst of the challenges of family building. We make mistakes, but God covers us and helps us walk through life with joy, love, and forgiveness.

Life is amazing, and God is always greater than our most dire circumstances that life may throw at us. We overcome all things by the power of the Spirit that flows in and through our lives. We are more than conquerors, no matter what!

Here I am, the dad. I want to tell you the things that my kids have done with me through the years. A lot surrounds the sports that they played: soccer (of course), T-ball, and basketball. Through the years, there have been very few games that I have missed, even up through high school. One time, I drove an hour and a half to get to Kaydee's basketball game. The game was twenty minutes long, and I was ten minutes late. Of the ten minutes I was able to watch, Kaydee played for two minutes. It was worth it.

When the boys were young (before Kaydee was born), I would take them to my job sites when I was building houses. I would often set my drill down to do something else, and it would be gone when I turned back around. Then I would find Samuel trying to use it on the wall, "just like Dad." He was about two.

Samuel, our oldest, started asking about his birth mom at the age of six. We talked about Miss Sylvia all the time and told him how much she loved him. As he got older, he began to ask when he could meet her. We told him that God would let us know when it was the right time. I just assumed it would be some time after high school. At age fifteen, we began to feel that God was saying it was time. We contacted Carol. She began the process that would lead to Samuel's first meeting with his birth mom.

Now, let me share some of what was going on in my mind and heart. I had, for lack of a better word, a "fear" that Samuel would like his birth mom so much that he would want to go live with her and his siblings. There were many questions that were answered through our time together that evening. They were "hows, whats, and whys" surrounding his adoption. It was just as important for Miss Sylvia. She and her other children are part of our family now. The reunion was as good for us as it was for him.

As I am writing this, Samuel is recovering from surgery on his ACL and meniscus. This has been very discouraging for him as he is pursuing a career as an athlete. It has been very important for me as his dad to be there for him and keep him encouraged.

Samuel thought back over his growing-up years. Here are some memories that his dad did for him that helped to mold him into the young man he is today. He remembered when he was two or three that his dad bought them matching shoes. Samuel said that whenever he wore those shoes, he felt he was as grown up as his dad. Samuel felt like he and his dad were twins. Through the years, he stated that his mom gave Samuel and Corey freedom to "do their thing." She did nurture him as she did all the siblings.

Dad always gave godly advice. Samuel knew his dad's advice was always for Samuel's good, and he needed to heed the truth because of his dad's wisdom and love. Early on, Samuel showed interest and skill in the sport soccer. Dad began working with Samuel in the backyard, showing him how to direct the ball where it would do the thing it was supposed to do. They spent hours playing with the soccer ball. Samuel said his dad was at every game. Samuel said his dad knows more than he, the son, knows. Dad also knows Samuel. He recognized that in his early years. This helped Samuel listen to Dad on many occasions when he selfishly wanted to do it his way. Dad walked Samuel through every difficulty successfully. He said his dad doesn't give up on Samuel's dream even more so than Samuel does. Another lesson Dad taught Samuel was how to stay true to himself, no matter what others think or say.

When Samuel was a young boy, he was involved with a group of potential soccer athletes. This meant that Samuel needed special athletic equipment. Dad put vending machines in several retail places to make extra money for the things Samuel would need. Samuel did play soccer professionally. Dad's vending machine business provided funds for Samuel to travel with the team to places before Samuel had worked his way to getting paid as a professional. Samuel traveled to Sweden, Greece, Iceland, Turkey, Belgium, Denmark, and England as a professional soccer athlete.

Samuel said his adoption was never hidden. It was always talked about as a positive, loving part of his life. Corey and Kristi adopted other children as well. That proved that each child had value as an individual and was a secure member of their family. Both Samuel's and Sylvia's families benefited from their meeting fifteen years after the placement. Sylvia had been fourteen at the time of Samuel's birth. The reason for her adoption choice for Samuel was she wanted him to have a mom *and* a dad. She certainly provided that for Samuel. It confirmed for Samuel what his parents had been showing him all his life was true. She wanted a dad for Samuel. Adoption was the only way she could provide that for her son.

This family's experiences of being "adopted into the family of God" has been the example they have followed in growing their children with that same security.

Corey is like the physical Pied Piper. His children would follow him to the moon and back, if that is where he's currently going.

NO LONGER ORPHANS

We had a beautiful family, but felt we had more love to give to a child who needed a mother and a father. We had always had a heart for adoption because Drew was adopted as an infant. His life was immensely blessed through adoption. His parents were beautiful people who gave him a home and a family he would not have had otherwise.

When we connected with Loving Alternative, we had no idea that God was preparing us, a birth mother, and a child for the adoption journey that lay ahead. Liam's birth mother shared that she wanted him to have a mother and a father, something she could not have given him. God knew that Liam would need Christian parents who could give him stability, love, and a solid foundation on which to grow.

Liam loves his family, but he has a special relationship with his dad, Drew. Just days before Liam was due, we got word from Fatherheart that the house parents were worried our birth mother might not follow through with placement. We were heartbroken, but knew that God had it under control. We prayed as a family and put it in God's hands. The next day, Drew heard from God. Drew was driving to work, and God solidified in his heart that Liam was his son. Even though Liam is adopted, this father and son are similar in many ways. They share adoption as part of their story. They love to fish, ride jet skis, look at cars, and enjoy ice cream cones!

Drew and Liam are most definitely a father-son duo. Drew taught Liam to fish, how to ride a bike, how to ride a lawn mower, and many more things. Liam could have probably done those things without a father, but know that during that teaching, Drew was putting way more in Liam than just a skill. He was teaching him to be a good person, a Godly person, and a person who could celebrate successes and be proud of himself!

Deana has mentioned that shortly before Liam's birth, there

was concern that the birth mother may change her mind regarding adoption. I will never forget the day as I was driving home praying about the situation. The Lord spoke to me in such a real way that I knew everything would be OK. After his birth, at the appropriate time, we dedicated Liam's life to the Lord. During the dedication portion of the church service, I got to pray a prayer of dedication and blessing over Liam. I will never forget that wonderful opportunity that I got to bless my son in front of our church body. I have included a copy of the prayer below, as I want others to hear the heart of a father as he publicly blessed his son.

>Liam Andrew, before you were born, I claimed you as my son. Today, I stand before God and these witnesses and publicly proclaim you as my son.
>
>Because of God's grace, love, and mercy, you have brought completeness to our family. Today, we stand here and thank Him for you and ask His blessings upon your life.
>
>May the Great Architect of the Universe whose spoken words created the world and the God before whom our fathers Abraham, Isaac, and Jacob walked, the God who has been our Shepherd to this day, and the Angel of the Lord who has redeemed us from all evil, bless you, Liam. Let the Name of the Lord be carried on through you. May your hands do the works of the Father; may your feet walk the paths that He has foreordained for you.
>
>May He create in you the desire to attend to His words, a willing and obedient heart that you may consent and submit to His sayings and walk in His ways. May the Lord bless you and keep you; may the Lord make His face shine upon you and be gracious to you; may He lift up His countenance upon you. And may you be filled with the light and the power of the Holy Spirit, in the Name of Yeshua the Messiah.

Liam has had a few struggles; however, he is a strong young man and has met those struggles with a lot of energy. His mother and I continue to love on him, encourage him, and pray for the Lord's will in his life. We have seen him grow and develop into a kindhearted, thoughtful, and gentle young man. I remember some of the questions that I had as a young adopted boy and have had the opportunity to share with him and encourage him when he has questions or thoughts that I would always be an open ear to hear. I am so thankful for the relationship that we have. I was honored on his eighth birthday when he relayed to Deana and me that he was interested in baptism and his relationship with the Lord. What a blessing to baptize Liam.

We enjoy a number of outside activities together. He is learning many "manly" things. We have been cutting trees, preparing flower beds, performing vehicle maintenance, and other such things. Additionally, we enjoy riding four wheelers, fishing, jet skiing, and watching the deer eat from our theater in our backyard. He has a soft heart for animals and loves our family dog.

I look forward to what the Lord has in store for Liam's life. Our family has been blessed with the opportunity to call him our son. I believe it is also our calling and responsibility to raise him. Deana has been such a wonderful mother to him, and I have been so blessed to be able to father him. Many blessings are in the future.

Pray with us for Liam's success in life and his ultimate call in the kingdom of God.

CHILDREN TELL THEIR STORIES

Here are just four powerful stories from adoptive children, now young adults. Each grew up with dads during all their formative years. Each is special and individual. From these very different situations, one can see how their "forever" dads will always be proud of the successful adults they are. They had the advantage of Dad and God working in partnership throughout those years. The foundations were formed and will remain permanently in future years because God is the same yesterday, today, and forever.

A LOVING ALTERNATIVE

I was saved from a life of brokenness. My birth mom grew up without a dad. There was no one to hold her, protect her, or tell her that she was valuable. So not knowing her value, she got pregnant. My mom wanted the absolute best for me. She didn't want me to end up like her, without a dad. So she fought and fought for me to have both a mom and a dad.

I was placed in a Christian family with parents who loved each other and me unconditionally. I believe God made women to want to be loved by men and God in a healthy way. That explains why little girls dress up and go twirl in front of their fathers and wait for their fathers to say, "Wow!" How beautiful you look today!"

As a little girl, I used to do that all the time. I would dress up in my little princess suit and go stand and wait for my dad to say something like "You look pretty today." I still blush even now when my dad says, "Gracie, you look pretty today."

I have to say that having a father in my life truly impacted and shaped me to be who I am today. As a young girl, I learned that my value doesn't come from boys; it comes from being made in the image of God. My dad played a significant role in teaching me that valuable lesson. Without a dad, I would be pregnant by now, or I would be broken and angry.

Growing up, my dad always was there to protect me. He was always there to hug me or tell me how beautiful I am. Dads have a key role in making the foundation of who their child is going to grow up to be. Most likely if there isn't a dad present, then kids get really messed up. I can see that evident in my life. I would always look to my dad to protect me.

When I was younger, I would be afraid if he wasn't home. My dad is one of the kindest, gentlest, selfless, and most Godly man that I have ever known. He never drinks. He is never immoral with other women. He always wanted the best for his kids. My dad is the one who is protective. He is the one who loves to share with me about Jesus. It always brightens his face to do so. If I didn't have him in my life, then I could get away with so much stuff and not care because no one would be there to tell me in a way that would make me stop. My mom obviously protects me and all that, but not like a dad. Not like *my* dad. My life would be so different, broken, and confusing if I didn't have a strong man figure called my dad in my life. I love my dad, and he is a part of what made me the me I am today.

***

The above was written by an adoptive daughter. She told about her dad and his involvement in her life. I want to add a postscript. Her dad was a staff member at our maternity home. He became like a hands-on dad to the girls residing in the home during their pregnancies. He is gifted as a dad. These girls found in this *dad* a closeness like the "real dad" they didn't have in their lives. Like Gracie, had they had a dad like hers, their lives could have been more like Gracie's. Perhaps they would have had a positive testimony and not have found themselves in the need of a time in a maternity home.

Dads do matter. They make a difference.

BONDING EXPERIENCES WITH MY DAD

Dad taught me how to ride a bike. Thinking of this brought to mind an unforgettable experience. We were riding bikes in the Green Acres parking lot. It was paved without bumps, and no cars were present. We didn't know we were breaking the law until, much to our surprise, a security guard approached. We were told to leave because we were on private property. That was as close as my dad and I were ever cited for breaking the law. I wasn't a bit afraid because I knew my dad was protecting me. The officer was only doing his job. We weren't even close to a jail sentence.

I used to roller-skate with both my parents around my neighborhood. My dad taught me how to fish. We'd go to Faulkner Park. Dad got me my own pink fishing rod. That gift made the "male" activity more feminine.

Dad taught me how to drive his truck at my Grampa's farm when I got my permit. He'd take me out to the farm where I'd hang out with him while he put the hay out for the animals.

Dad and I went to all the dad-and-daughter events that my school held throughout the years. There were dances, formal events, and donut/hot chocolate parties.

One time I wanted to have a Christmas party for my dad. I asked my mom to make it a fancy party with fancy food. She is a good cook, so it was fun for me to help her make this event extra special with some of Dad's favorites. Then we got all dressed up for the party so he'd be surprised when he came in the door from work. Delight showed on his face. It turned out to be an unexpected celebration. I'm definitely a Daddy's girl.

SECURITY VS. REJECTION

When I get to meet a pregnant girl, I always emphasize the baby in the womb. That mom needs to talk to the baby, love the baby, pray for the baby, and read little stories to the baby like she would do if the baby were in her arms. She should give the baby a name and call him or her by that name. Early on, one of our birth moms taught this to me. She was about five months along when she called again after having come in very early in her pregnancy. She said, "I'm so glad a pregnancy is nine months long. If it had only been four or five months, I would have parented. But I had those extra months to learn what God wanted me to do. I learned He had an adoption plan for my son. So I thought, 'What would I do if he were in my arms? I would do [all the things I mentioned above].'"

And she did for those next four or five months. She placed that baby boy with a family. We keep in touch with the family and the child and the birth mom for many months and even years. That boy has grown into the most secure person one would ever meet. He doesn't know the meaning of the word *rejection*. If he goes door to door to collect for scouts—or any other reason—and they hesitate or even say something like, "Not now. Come back later," he does go back later, always with a good attitude. If he has to go back several times, he does until they give.

That is just one example that shows his security and what that love in the womb can do for a baby. Now when I work with a birth mom, I always ask how she feels about her baby. Then I teach her to love that baby in the womb with all the above connections. I don't leave it there. I emphasize her desire for that baby to have security no matter if she parents or if she chooses adoption for that child. When we meet routinely, I go over those tasks with her again. If the birth mom doesn't want the baby, or she doesn't bond with that child in the womb, a "spirit of rejection" can become a reality in that child. That child will unintentionally sabotage successes throughout his life regardless of his abilities, personality, and intelligence. This can be prayed out of him if the parents recognize the situation and the connection they all have with the healing Spirit of God.

Below is the story from the secure boy, now an adult young man. He had a double dose of the positive impact in his life.

***

Early Childhood
My dad was the role model I looked up to. With him being in the home and involved with my life, I got to see what it meant to be a godly man. It is hard to pick a specific story because growing up with him, I was surrounded by his love and godly instruction.

He would take time out of his day to work with me with my Awana club. He helped me understand what the Bible had to say about my life and how God had loved me since before I was born.

He taught me how to overcome challenges by myself and try to figure out problems and solutions and not have others do the work for me. I especially remember making a pinewood derby car for Cub Scouts. I had to build it by myself, but he was there to support me and give advice. He really showed me how to be a man. There were times that he let me fail, but he was there to show me how to overcome the failure next time.

My father walked with me during my leg surgeries in both the literal and spiritual sense. My dad molded me into a man of God that now, as I live my life, I still fall back on his teachings. Now that I have a daughter of my own, I pass down the blessing God used my father to bestow on me. I spend quality time with my daughter as I attempt to bestow those characteristics on her.

***

His birth mom could have been a great mom. During her pregnancy, she proved she was a nurturer. Her love for Caleb in the womb prepared him for greatness growing up to manhood. She could never have filled the role of a dad. His job is to be the spiritual leader, the provider, and the protector. The family who parented Caleb filled their roles perfectly. Caleb is proof of that as he has no signs of rejection in his spirit. It began in the womb, but continued in his physical and spiritual life.

MOM'S STORIES

In many families, dads are busy being dads. This means they are the priests in the home, the provider, the protector, and the playmate. The moms are behind the scenes, nurturing and supporting the dads' discipline methods with *love*.

You may recall during school, girls were studious and communicative. It follows that these stories written by moms show a continuation of those traits in these women in their current role as moms.

I think you'll feel the passion of the moms to nurture is evident in their stories. Aren't you glad in God's design for families, He chose moms *and* dads?

TWO PARENTS GIVE POSITIVE EXAMPLES TO FOLLOW

I'm Ben. I was placed into my "forever family" as a baby twenty years ago. I'm glad I had the parents God gave me. I am glad I had a dad and a mom.

I've known friends who had to do the things I never experienced. They had to go back and forth between their mom and dad because the parents were no longer living together.

The kids had to balance their time between each parent. Children in cases like this may feel insecure.

My dad taught me many things that my mom couldn't have taught me. Here are some examples: car repair, shooting guns, handling knives, building fires, carpentry, and cutting down trees. Mom was always there behind the scenes, cheering us on.

Because my mom and dad had a good loving marriage, they showed me what a good marriage looks like. Dad was an example of how to be a good husband and father. I want to be like him.

TOGETHERNESS

How is it possible that twenty-three years have passed since our precious daughter came into our lives? She was three days old when her birth mother so lovingly placed her in our arms. It was an emotional day and one that I'll never forget. Her birth mom was so young, so mature, and so selfless in her gift of life to our family. When we left the maternity home, I felt like we had taken the heart of our birth mother with us that day. We've never forgotten that moment, and we vowed that the sacrifice she made would always be honored in our home.

Our daughter brought us such joy over the years. Besides being absolutely adorable and beautiful, she brought us laughter and love. Our son (adopted nine years earlier) was the best big brother! He taught her all about sports, bike riding, climbing trees, and taking care of pet tarantulas and pet snakes! She loved her brother with all her heart and wanted to follow in his footsteps. To this day, the two of them remain very close!

As sweet and fun as growing up was for the first fifteen years, the older teenage years were tough and challenging! Thank goodness that together, my husband and I were able to love her through those times. It took both of us, including an army of prayer warriors, to see her through to the mature woman, wife, and mother that she is today! We couldn't be more proud than when we see her with her own family, making decisions based on her upbringing. Turns out that she really was listening during those teen years! God is so good!

Within the past two years, she has been reunited with her birth mother and has met her birth father too! She maintains a very positive relationship with both of them, and this has brought a sense of peace for her and enlarged our circle of family members!

I recently had the opportunity to talk to our daughter about our family. As our daughter talked about growing up, I came to realize what an important role my husband has in her life. She mentioned words such as *love, safety, responsibility, self-respect,* and *humility*. She told me, "Dad always made me feel secure. I know with 100 percent confidence, he will always be there for me." This reminded me of a time that she and I helped drive our son's Boy Scout troop to Colorado for summer camp. We dropped them off in southern Colorado, and then we went camping ourselves right outside of Colorado Springs. We still refer to this as our "Barbie goes camping" trip. We set up the tent with Barbie sheets, Barbie blanket, and had a Barbie camping lantern. She had a Barbie toothbrush and Barbie pajamas too! But at night, she was frightened to be alone without Daddy. Luckily, she also had a make-believe Barbie phone. All I needed to tell her was, "Hold on to this phone, and if anything happens, we'll call Daddy right away!" She slept with her phone held tightly every night with a sense of security that only a daddy can provide.

She talked about how Daddy was different from me. I know that I can talk about anything and explain things thoroughly, but she said, "Dad doesn't say a lot and chooses his words very carefully, so when he talks, I listen." She also mentioned that he's very humble about his accomplishments, and she respects him for the quiet way he lives his life with integrity. Maybe she needed both of our styles, but this may be a good lesson in "less is more."

She also talked about how we supported her interests and that she got to at least experience trying any and every sport or activity that she was interested in. She made a list for me that included the following: gymnastics, cheer, ice-skating, dance, soccer, track, volleyball, cross country, baseball, tennis, Girl Scouts, summer camps, summer clubs, science clubs, and swimming. She mentioned that when she wanted to play volleyball that Dad put up a volleyball net for her in the backyard to help her practice. When she thought that soccer would be fun but it wasn't for her, Dad made her stick with her commitment to her team through the end of the season. She was such a good soccer player that we thought for sure this would be her sport! Before we knew it though, she was on to something new. These were such great years that lasted all the way until she got her driver's license, and she no longer needed so much parental involvement. It was hard to step back and let her experience some independence, but that too is part of growing up.

Can we just skip the teenage years and fast-forward to her wedding day? It was springtime and a beautiful day. There was our precious daughter ready to marry her prince charming. There were tears when my husband saw her in her wedding dress for the first time. She was more than beautiful, and she was so happy! As I watched my husband walk our daughter down the aisle, I knew there was nothing but pure love in his heart for the gift he was giving to our son-in-law. I wonder if this is the feeling her birth mother had so many years ago? Love came full circle on that day.

A STRONG DAD MAKES STRONG KIDS/ADULTS

Almost every day I am reminded of the role both a mother and father play in the life of our children. Statistics show that children from a single-parent home are five to ten times more likely to fall into drug use, premarital sex, trouble with the law, and perform poorly at school. I believe choosing a home with a mother and a father was perhaps the most important factor in motivating our birth moms to choose adoption for their two precious children.

Our children are now leaving the nest, going to college, and starting their careers. Dad was always an important and needed person in their lives, but wow, he has become extremely important to them in the more recent years. He has always provided the strength and toughness they needed. Left with just me, I would have babied them and possibly pitied them from the tough issues in life. He always encouraged them to face their fears knowing God was with them. But with just a dad, they wouldn't have had the shoulder to cry on when things went sour.

When their car broke down or they had their first fender bender, they called Dad. When their first girlfriend/boyfriend trouble came, they reached out to me. Dad built the diving platform in the tree over the pond out back. I provided the ice-cold popsicles. Dad taught them how to work hard, run a tractor, keep a Weed eater going, and chop firewood. I kept the hot chocolate flowing in the cold temperatures. Dad confronted issues with school teachers and coaches. I drove them to and from school and helped them with all their school projects. Dad used his influence to help them secure their first jobs. I listened to their woes after a long day at work. Dad provided a stable income. I provided a warm home environment with clean clothes and good meals.

There were times when Dad was exhausted from a long day at work, and I picked up all the slack with the kids. Other times I was overcome by a migraine, and Dad took care of every detail, from dinner to schoolwork. I can't imagine the stress single parents must be under to be on call at all times.

Just recently, our daughter had a young man interested in her. Dad met him, took him aside, and asked him some pertinent questions and discovered he was masking some serious issues. Dad saved our daughter from a most certain future heartache. Only a father can really play this important role.

We've spent long hours into the night discussing issues facing our children. God uniquely equips a woman with a caring heart. God uniquely equips a man with a logical mind. Together we make a team best suited to provide the guidance our children needed and still need. Many times, I would comment, "These kids are fortunate to have a father because I would not have been wise enough to make a good decision here." Other times, Dad would comment, "These kids are fortunate to have a mother as I would never do as much for them as you do."

The early years with our children really called on me as a mother most of all. Dad was important back then, but as they started into adolescents, his influence became more and more needed. As young adults, they call on him all the time for varied needs.

God's creation is amazing. His creation of the family is amazing. The way males/dads and females/moms complement each other is amazing. Adoption is amazing in how it takes a child born out of the family structure and places that child within a family structure they so desperately need.

Our daughter is doing amazingly well! Just went back to college yesterday. She has worked hard all summer at the health food store and has saved almost every dime. She is saving up to pay for a semester of study at Oxford in England. She is working toward getting her bachelor's and master's at the same time. She is beyond precious—a total joy! And she has the most amazing sense of humor. She keeps us laughing.

Mom and Dad have worked together parenting these two precious children. However, it was God's continual loving guidance that gets the credit for the success that is evident in the lives of this whole family. God is so good.

DADS PLUS DAUGHTERS EQUALS BEAUTY

"Every adopted child is a child born of trauma—even if adopted at birth." I remember hearing those words in our training. I remember the day Carol told us that we are raising Madelyn to be strong and have the tools to overcome, but her story will always have ugly parts. I look often at the painting in Madelyn's room from her birth mom with a note on the back that explains how the lotus is a beautiful flower that blooms despite growing from dark and murky swamp water. Madelyn's life did begin with trauma, and there will always be parts we all wish were different. We have to remember that and parent with compassion. The older she gets, though, the more her life diverges from the murky waters of the one it could have been, and the more it becomes the life her mom prayed it would be.

Like every child, the older Madelyn gets, the more we see her unique personality. We see the tendencies and traits that she didn't learn from us but are inherent. I can't count how many times I catch David looking at her nostalgically and saying, "She looks just like [her mom] when she does that." There are parts of Madelyn we can give to her and parts that we have to learn about her and parent accordingly.

Maddie is a pleaser. She wants to know that we, as her parents, are happy with her. If our tone is too harsh when disciplining, she sometimes caves in on herself. Unlike my older strong-willed daughter, Madelyn does not respond with defiance (a trait I think she gets from her birth mom). She reacts by assuming the bad choice makes her a bad person. In those moments, I look in those deep brown eyes and know that if I were to misuse my power as her parent, I could make Madelyn do just about anything. That thought is literally bone-chilling.

Madelyn's birth father made some grievous mistakes. If her birth mom had not taken the incredibly brave stand that she did, Madelyn would almost certainly have been a victim by this point in her life. And the abuse would have been ongoing because she would do anything to earn the love of those she needs most.

While she aims to please, Maddie also has a quick temper. Those two things seem opposed, but they are two sides of the same coin. When something doesn't go her way, she responds to her parents with resignation, but she responds to her sister and peers with anger. She lashes out, physically hitting, kicking, pinching, or biting. Her natural inherent reaction is aggression. If you didn't know her intimately, in those moments, you would assume she was intentionally hurting others rather than responding to her own hurt. It would appear she was attacking someone else, while in reality, she was attempting to protect herself. As parents, we do know Madelyn intimately, so we teach her better ways to cope. In a different environment with less oversight and/or stronger triggers, Madelyn's temper could dictate her actions.

Madelyn is tough as nails, especially when she's in the wrong. She is a follower and wants to be accepted. Her height, strength, and stature make her appear much older than she is. She is sensitive to a fault. All those traits and more would have had a very different outcome in a different context. David and I are constantly, intentionally aware of those possibilities, and we lead her accordingly.

We don't dwell, but we never want to forget what could have been Madelyn's life. We purposely keep that picture in our minds because it's a part of who Madelyn is. To deny or ignore that would be to overlook a piece of who she is.

Madelyn is not a victim. Her father, rather than taking from her, gives her more than she could ask or imagine. He affirms who she is, and because of that, she is learning she doesn't have to do anything to please us.

David was out of town recently, and Madelyn wanted to have a dance party. (That means she wants to dress up like a princess and do her version of a ballet/ballroom number.) I wasn't able to stop what I was doing, and when I told her no, she looked sad for a brief moment and then said, "It's okay. Daddy will dance with me when he gets home. Daddy always dances with me." There was no question in her mind that he'd make time and want to join her. She knows that he loves her so much that he would dance with her anytime, anyplace.

Because he has. She knows she is valuable because he shows her. She's learning that's how God sees her because David is modeling unconditional love and acceptance.

Last week in the midst of an argument with her sister, Madelyn started to lash out. You could see the tension in her little heart as she gritted her teeth and steeled her eyes, but she stopped herself from doing what felt natural and chose to do what's right. David encouraged her to make a good choice, and after some serious consideration, she grabbed his hand and told her sister she was sorry. Then she ran and burrowed herself in her daddy's lap. Madelyn is learning that she's strong enough to do hard things because her dad is there to hold her hand and encourage her as she does.

Madelyn has no interest in riding a bike. She has a large trike that she loves, but when a family bike ride is suggested, she doesn't want to ride next to her sister or behind me. She wants to sit on the seat attached to David's bike. Made for a small toddler, the seat sits between David and the handlebars, so David's arms are on both sides of her as they ride. Although she outgrew it a long time ago, that seat is her favorite place to be—right there, between her daddy's arms. She feels the comfort of his protection and the freedom to simply enjoy the ride. From the moment they get on the bike to the moment they get off (and then some), she talks to her dad. She tells him stories (real and imagined), points out things to see, and navigates the way.

There's no mistaking that Madelyn's life looks different than it could have. But in addition to how it looks, more important is that Madelyn's heart is different. Having a dad to depend on, learn from, and take comfort in are great things. The bigger thing, however, is that every time David exhibits those traits of unconditional love, unquestioned worth, and unending protection, Madelyn sees a little more of God's character. Anyone who knows Jesus knows what it means to have a life that could have been. Madelyn is the walking, talking evidence of when His Grace intersects a path, everything changes.

SURPRISE! TWIN BABY GIRLS

Everything is easier and better when there are two people to share the "burdens" (and joys) of parenting, especially with twins. Parents can be such a help and an encouragement for each other.

Each of us has parenting skills that the other does not have.

I, Mom, was able to stay at home and raise and nurture these two babies. Later, I was able to be very involved with their schooling. I was a room mom, chaperone, and volunteer.

We, as a couple, offered financial stability. All their needs were met, including all medical needs. There were times when we chose to pay certain medical specialists who were not within our insurance plan because we wanted to ensure expert care. They were able to attend the out-of-state colleges of their choice, get engineering degrees, and complete college with no debt.

Dad showed the girls what a Godly husband looks like by the way he has treated me, the Mom, with love, kindness, respect, and faithfulness. All that caused my *joy* tank to overflow all these years.

The twins entered functional extended family settings with loving relatives on both sides. Our daughters had a normal, secure upbringing when so many other children, adopted or not, are living in insecurity, fear, and possibly hunger.

Having their godly father in the picture gave them many blessings.

Dad's unconditional love for them reflected God's love for all of us. He lived the proper physical attention that daughters need by freely expressing his love. His calm, wise, godly spirit offered security. He was present at all school and extracurricular and church functions, including teaching Sunday school and being an Awana leader. His chaperone presence caused the girls to look at Dad and not for another "male" companion. He was a father who was never too tired for them and even ran any last-minute errands they asked of him. His wisdom and knowledge helped the girls with the hard school subjects as well as any financial matters.

When it came time to select college, he ironed out all the details that entailed in ways they could understand, pros and cons of the various schools.

Altogether, he was a fully involved dad to these precious twin daughters. Because he lovingly fulfilled all the tasks assigned to the dad, these twin girls have become beautiful women inside and out. The example that Dad was in their lives might make it difficult for them to find a life mate with such high standards he modeled.

As the girls reached the age when they began to see boys from a different light than they did in their younger years, they noticed the boys were looking at them differently too. Because their dad was such a positive influence in their lives, the girls knew any boy who wanted to be serious with them needed to pass the "okay" of their dad. This dad was a built-in "protector" for the girls in every area of their lives. They as well as their dad were confident that God would guide them to the partner God chose for their future lives— and the right father of their children.

MOM IS HALF THE TEAM

Two parents are better than one in almost every family. Two opinions on every aspect of raising a child help the parents chart the best course to direct the child. Two very different perspectives guide, teach, and equip both parents for better in their separate as well as their partnership in parenting. Two parents are able to encourage each other, resulting in successful parenting.

Christianity in the home is key in this family's togetherness. Prayer and dependence on God develop a child's character and helps the whole family cope with issues that will inevitably arise in life.

Our family's prayers have helped their lives be an example to other couples. We found prayer was essential to develop a tight family. We pray that others will see our bonded family members and attempt to do the same in their family. We experienced our involvement in church enforced a Christian worldview that helped our daughter have stability as it established a basic foundation of morality.

We balanced our activities around sports, including soccer, basketball, tennis, and softball. Travel and vacations were another thing that were included in giving balance with variety. Rachel even took a short-term mission trip to Uganda. The arts and music through piano, guitar, violin, and dance lessons helped to round out Rachel's interest. We found that Rachel was very talented in these areas. Concerts and shows of different kinds were included in Rachel's upbringing.

Even in hard economic times, we made it through. We both worked hard and were able to provide a private Christian school education for Rachel. She was never in day care.

I stayed home when Rachel was young and then went to work to pay for education when Rachel started school.

One or both of us parents were at every event she was involved in her entire life. She got support and encouragement every step along the way. Our involvement showed Rachel our ever-present love.

DAD BRINGS COHERENCY

Rusty is my husband and the dad in this family. He has been a true example of Christ. Rusty has always shown the boys unconditional love, even when their choices could have been more godly. He has always given unselfishly to help the boys reach their goals.

Our family would not be complete without Jaxon. The best times are watching the boys grow together. Jaxon and Gramm have never known what it feels like to be insecure due to a lack of having a father. Rusty has always made sure they both have all they need financially and emotionally.

The boys love doing things together. When Jaxon was younger, Rusty coached him in baseball. Watching Rusty, Jaxon, and Gramm out in the yard practicing together was better than watching the games.

We don't get to do it as much as we'd like due to crazy schedules, but we love playing games. It's fun to see the boys be competitive and still be able to lose with laughter and not take each other too seriously.

Jaxon and Gramm love listening to books together when they travel to practice or away games. Gramm is a questioner. He asks very deep questions that Rusty always loves discussing. Only recently is "how the Lord gives us more than we can handle." Through these discussions, the lesson learned is if it's too much for us to handle alone, we learn the need to always look to God. We always see God's plan working out for the best.

Now both boys work on fixing Jaxon's truck and adding things to it for Jaxon's part-time job. That job is hauling metal and helping people with odd jobs. Jaxon has a jack-of-all-trades personality. He also has a weekend job at the local BBQ place in town. We've learned that letting him try a lot of different things teaches him a lot. He's found he is quite well rounded.

Jaxon loves both jobs. One, because he loves his boss, and the other because he is the boss. Either way, he always surprises us with some good BBQ or some great find from someone's trash pile. He is currently building his own smoker and has smoked some wonderful brisket for us.

Gramm and Rusty really like working on math problems together. When Gramm can't figure out a problem, he and Rusty discuss it together. Recently they just drew out a plan for the Christmas lights on the house. They did measurements for all the items they'd need. Mom just watched.

Both boys, along with Dad, love building things. Jaxon is more of a "throw it together and it just works" guy. Gramm and Rusty like to have a plan. Actually, all three of the "guys" like to research and then see how it works out.

Rusty and Gramm like riddles and jokes between the two of them. Mom says most of the riddles are way above her brain and capacity. She lets them have their fun.

Jaxon also plays the saxophone in the school band. This means the family enjoys an impromptu concert every once in a while.

While Jaxon is a natural athlete and could have a college scholarship and possibly play in the major leagues as a pitcher, that hasn't been where he wants to devote his time. At 6'6", he is every basketball coach's dream, but Jaxon loves playing the saxophone. This meant we did what was needed to help him pursue that dream. Neither Dad nor Mom had band parents, nor did they find being at band concerts a natural pastime. However, because Jaxon loves it, we go to the games and sit in the band section wearing our band T-shirts.

Jaxon is also a hard worker. This summer, Rusty spent time and money to help him get the tools and equipment he needed to start his scrap metal business. Never in a million years would we have thought we'd be giving him the tools to start the scrap metal business. We'd always dreamed of him playing baseball and going to college.

Who's to say he won't change his mind and go to college on a baseball scholarship, but instead of shutting his ideas down, Rusty always encourages him.

Jaxon has always been very busy. The need for Rusty and me to work together in raising the boys has been helpful for us to be able to rest while the other takes over. There are also things Mom has no way of knowing what to do or how to handle, Rusty knows, and vice versa. I cannot imagine trying to parent without the support of my husband, the boys' dad. When I'm at the end of my rope, there is someone to tag-team with. Rusty is quick to teach the boys how never to belittle me for my weaknesses. He teaches the boys to protect me as a woman. Yet he never makes me feel like I'm lesser.

I've wanted to keep this positive, but the truth is kids are going to make bad choices. Jaxon has admitted he likes to see what happens when he "crosses" the boundaries we set in place. This has led to many sleepless nights. Rusty has always been a rock! Yes, there has been yelling, LOL. Rusty always uses these trying times to redirect Jaxon. The goal is always to teach Jaxon the consequences of his actions and hold him accountable while extending a lot more grace than I alone would give.

I as Mom am now in more of a support role. I make sure all are fed and clothed and the guys know how to do these things if I am not available. But I still love that Jaxon comes to me when he needs personal help. Like the time he got poison ivy or just wanted or needed to talk. He still hugs and kisses me and even sends random texts telling me he loves me. He even bought a Mother's Day present with his own money and didn't tell anyone. Both, of course, made my day.

Now that the boys are getting older, I see Rusty teaching both boys how to be men. I also see these lessons taking root in how Rusty treats me, the mom, in word and deeds. However, they will always be my little boys.

Even at this crazy time, while we are both on furlough and the future is unsure, Rusty continues to use this time with the boys, letting them know we can trust the Lord. When they come to him, he takes the time to help them pursue their dreams, all the while pointing them to Jesus.

This dad, Rusty, is a real example to the boys not only what a godly man/dad is like, but also how to respect and honor the woman in their family —Mom. They've been groomed for manhood by an exceptional dad.

SERVICE IS THIS FAMILY'S MIDDLE NAME

AJ said that he loves his relationship with his dad. The times they've spend fishing together is his favorite. As he's approaching fourteen (crazy!), he longs for that time, just him and his dad. This summer, they actually got the blessing of going on a guys' fly-fishing trip to Colorado for five days! Our youth pastor and his adopted son, Brady, were there too, and it will be a trip he never forgets! The bonding, the trust, the connection they have is just priceless. I think it's probably going to be a yearly thing now.

Some of our favorite family times are on the construction mission trips each summer. Paige and AJ both see their mom and dad serve for our "summer vacation" and is just such a blessing. They look forward to it every year. Celebrating the Fourth of July each year all over the country is another memorable event. We go the same week every summer. We've built so many sweet memories!

AJ looks forward to being sixteen, when he will be allowed to work on site with his dad—building and serving wherever God directs.

Both children help in the kitchen at church each summer. When on our mission trips each summer, our kids often help with the younger kids whose parents are working. They are both such great servants. I praise the Lord that He has given us these opportunities to serve and allow our kids to serve with us as a family.

Paige Ann loves her daddy-daughter dance each February around Valentine's Day. She and I go together and find a special dress. Dad brings her flowers and just showers her with sweet love. We also were blessed to lead her to the Lord this past year! We were all together at home. She prayed with us to receive Christ as her Savior. That was a special moment for all four of us.

I think some of their most treasured times with both parents are our evening devotions. We have used Louie Giglio's devotional books for families focused around science, which is important for AJ. He is very into science. We want to nurture that so that he has a solid foundation of creation. We read together and save our Christmas cards each year so we can pray over a different family each night. This is another sweet time.

There is a security and stability I know they feel by having a mom and a dad. They each need different things from each of us at different times in their growth.

As we look around for solid families, we are finding them fewer in number. Why are families broken more and more? That problem is often answered by one word—*selfishness*. This family shows strength built on the slogan of some years ago. He came to serve and not to be served. The example of Jesus and his Father shows a tightness that'll keep this family from brokenness.

ADOPTED BY THE COMMUNITY

We have a close relationship with the members of our community. I, the mom, have taught in the high school for years. Many of the students are now adults and continue to live in our town. My husband, the dad, is a practicing lawyer in our town. Our family has deep roots in the community. As we began the process of adoption, the entire community kept close tabs on the process. June Ji came to us from China in 2003. The whole community had been praying for us. When she finally joined our family, it was as if she'd been adopted by every family in town. She has been such a blessing to us and our community.

We desired a daughter because we had three sons. To this day, we always comment on how perfectly she fit into our family. I, her mother, loved my sons but desired a relationship with a daughter. I have a close relationship with my own mother and wanted that same type of bond with a daughter. God heard my prayer, and He gifted me with June Ji. She and I are quite close. I am close to my sons as well, but my relationship with her is different. We do a lot of things together that my sons would not care to do. Girl things fit both June Ji and me. We shop, travel, walk, and enjoy so many other "girl" things. As of now, she is working on receiving her bachelor's degree from Texas A&M with the excitement of beginning a teaching career with elementary-age children. Pretty exciting.

June Ji also has a strong bond with her dad. He offers different things from what I can. She looks to him for good advice. His logical mind does that. I remember when she was sixteen and had just received her driver's license. She left for a friend's house at night and miscalculated a turn. She ended up in the ditch and called dad to rescue her. She knew that I would not know the first thing of what to do, but she trusted her dad. This was emphasized again this past January when, leaving for class early one morning, she ran into a cow that was in the middle of the road. She happened to be driving my car as hers was in the shop. She told me that her first thought was to call her dad. He would know what to do.

God has gifted each of us with different qualities as He made both male and female. I offer a tender heart to both my boys and my daughter. Her dad offers practical advice. He is the spiritual leader, the provider, the protector, and often the playmate. We now have two granddaughters, two grandsons, and a third granddaughter on the way. We continue to see those differences as we embrace these grandchildren who have blessed our lives tremendously. June Ji is our youngest, and we are excited to see what the future holds for her. She is deeply loved by her two brothers and her brothers' wives. She is quite close to both of them and is able to understand what having a sister feels like. She adores her nieces and nephews and honestly cannot wait to one day have a family of her own. We are excited to see God work in that area too.

She has often stated that she has been blessed all these years with a full family. She has a mom, a dad, and brothers. Now sisters-in-law as well as nieces and nephews have been added. Each one of these are gifts she doesn't remember having in her original country. She really is loved in this full family.

June Ji's original family lived in China. In the years of her young life there, girls had very little value. Girls were put on the adoption market because China had an overpopulation problem.

Their theory was to send the girls out of the country as a plan to slow down the population growth. This introduced a spirit of abandonment for girls. They felt worthless. In June Ji's case and adoption, she gained real security, value, and worth with a dad and a mom in a community with folks who welcomed her, prayed for her, and loved her.

IT'S ALL ABOUT FAITH

As we sit and watch Faith play with the LOL dolls and accessories that her birth mother sent to her this week through the agency, we marvel at all that has occurred to get us to this place in our lives with a beautiful nine-year-old who is our love and joy.

We, like many other couples, were devastated when we realized that we couldn't have children. We began to research agencies and now know, without a doubt, that God led us to the Loving Alternative Adoption Agency where He knew our future daughter would be. We went through the usual paperwork, orientation, visits, and all that is required in the adoption process. We were thrilled beyond words when we got the call that the birth mom had chosen us to parent the precious baby who she would soon have.

Meeting the birth mother was very humbling as we realized the sacrifice she was making because of her love and concern for her child. We understand adoption because Hayden is adopted. He knows the feelings of an adopted child and is able to help Faith relate to circumstances that surface in her life.

Faith has known from the beginning that she is adopted. She knows that her birth mother and birth father live in another state. She realizes that the gifts that come at Christmas and birthdays are from them. She also knows that her adoptive father is adopted just like she is, and that he has not met his birth parents. On the other hand, she has an aunt who is adopted and who met her birth parents when she was nineteen years old. She has had a relationship with them for many years.

This knowledge has helped Faith with some of the questions that are in the mind of an adopted child. Faith understands that someday she will be able to meet her birth parents if she chooses. We have raised Faith in a Christian home, teaching her the principles of love. God has given her a heart big enough to be filled with the love of many people.

Faith's birth family remains connected using the adoption agency as the middle man. We send pictures and updates through the agency. We get gifts, letters, and correspond from the birth family through the ministry as well. We asked the birth dad for his family history as we were making a family tree for Faith. As we are putting together the family tree, Faith is feeling that her birth parents care about her well-being. This has given her a sense of security and peace. She knows that Hayden is her dad. They have a wonderful close bond. He'd do anything to protect her and show his love. He instinctively knows what will give Faith security as he has lived being adopted all his life. He has had no connection with his birth family. When he was placed for adoption those years ago, adoptions were done so differently. Today, knowledge of the emotional needs of these children is more widely known. Adoptive children are much healthier than they were years ago. We are all grateful.

These nine years have flown by. Faith is growing into a lovely young lady who makes us, her parents, proud. She has a "village" of people around her who love and support her. We are so thankful that God chose her birth parents to "give her life" and is using us, her adoptive parents, "to show her how to live it."

EXPLORING SUMMER

"I want to go home," our oldest daughter, seven-year-old Gracie, cried. We had just arrived at our annual summer vacation spot, a beautiful lake in the northern United States near Canada. We'd driven over twenty hours to see Grandma and Grandpa. And though we'd visited their grandparents at the lake every year since we'd adopted Gracie at birth, it was the first year our daughters were old enough for our family to stay in the nearby little cabin. Their beds, accessed by climbing a ladder into a loft, were new and different for our girls.

"I miss Harvey," said three-year-old Ava, tears brimming for our beloved family dog. He was staying with friends.

I did my best to encourage the girls with reminders of the fun they'd had in years past. "You'll fish with Grandpa and eat Grandma's caramel rolls and swim in the lake and go on boat rides and have a campfire and toast marshmallows. You're going to have so much fun!"

Gracie gave a begrudging nod. Ava sniffed. Both girls seemed hopeful, but not entirely convinced the adventures ahead of us were promising.

Their dad and I said prayers, sang bedtime songs, and tucked the girls into bed.

"Tomorrow is going to be a great day," their dad, Joe, said. "Let's get a good night's sleep so we can have lots of fun."

The next morning, the girls bounced out of their pajamas and into shorts and shirts, ready to take on the day. Their concerns from the night before seemed to have vanished into the bright blue sky greeting us. Wearing life vests, they headed toward the lakeshore. Near the dock, a shallow pool had been partitioned from the rest of the lake with rocks piled in a row. The rocks extended like a bridge to a small patch of land the family fondly called Blueberry Island.

Ava noticed something move in the clear water. Her little fingers pointed. "What's that?"

"That's a crayfish," Joe said. "We've got some nets and a bucket. We can catch them."

A questioning expression crossed Ava's face. Some of the crayfish were small, but others boasted large pinchers from crevices in the rocks.

Gracie took a careful step into the water, using her net as a walking stick. Ava stood on the sidelines, watching her big sister scout the area. Joe allowed the girls to explore for themselves, while giving some fatherly wisdom and advice.

"When I was a kid, my brothers, sister, and I would spend hours catching crayfish in this very spot," he said. "The crayfish will try to escape by scooting backward, so you'll want to place the nets behind them to scoop them up."

I stood by armed with sunscreen, bug spray, towels, water bottles, and snacks—the standard supplies for moms. But I had no good advice on how to best catch crayfish.

"You've got to be quiet, and then quick," Joe advised.

Gracie's first few attempts resulted in empty nets, but Joe and I gently encouraged her. "Keep at it. You can do it."

A sudden squeal pierced the air. "I caught one!" Gracie ran toward us with a crayfish clinging to the inside of her net.

"Wowzers!" I exclaimed. "That's a big one—almost a mini lobster!"

Ava, now convinced catching one of these strange creatures was possible, joined in with "I want one! I want one!"

After catching a bucketful of crawfish in the shallow pool, their sights expanded to Blueberry Island. But the girls' wide eyes and hesitant steps told us that crossing the rocks seemed a daunting task. Their dad knew only fun and adventure awaited.

"The rocks are firm. They'll hold you," Joe advised Gracie. "Place your foot on one, then take a step. You got it. Now put your foot on that large flat one. There you go."

Three-year-old Ava needed a little more assistance. Joe took her little hand in his and helped her find her footing along the rocks. With each step, the girls' confidence grew. Soon, they were both scrambling along the rock path, laughing. With Dad leading the way, the girls successfully made it to Blueberry Island and back. Their faces beamed with pride at their achievement.

That night, after releasing the crayfish back to the pond and enjoying hot dogs and toasted marshmallows at a campfire, the girls snuggled into their beds. Gone were the fears and sadness of the night before, replaced by good memories and a sense of pride and accomplishment.

The rest of the vacation was explored with confidence as the girls swam and tubed in the lake, caught frogs and grasshoppers, "drove" the boat with Grandpa, fished for minnows, helped build campfires, spotted deer and fawns, walked nature trails, and more. The early guidance and support provided a strong foundation for both girls to grow and take on new adventures—a summer vacation success!

***

This couple was blessed twice to be adoptive parents to babies who are now their amazing daughters. Gracie is seven, and Ava is three.

Vacations or ordinary living at home and school have all been made into adventures for these sisters because their dad Joe and their mom make it so. This dad does make a difference in the secure, happy lives of these sisters.

HEAVENLY FATHER HELPS DAD

I was thinking of all the advantages my children have because they have their dad.

My kids have a dad who can fix almost anything. Whenever something is broken, their first thought is *Where is Dad?* He has helped them with broken backpacks, bikes, cars, and even electronic stuff. It has been a huge blessing to have someone to go to with all their "fix it" problems! It has also prepared them to know that they can run to their Heavenly Father with things that are broken in their lives.

My children also have a dad who is a networker and knows a lot of people in our community. He has been able to "put in a good word" for all of them in various ways that has helped them get jobs or positions that have helped them out. Without his speaking up for them, they would have missed many opportunities.

Their dad also has a good reputation and is known as someone who is trustworthy in our community. In turn, people know our kids are responsible and trustworthy.

They have also learned to be generous with finances and their time by watching their father serve and help people.

There are also the obvious things, like our children have had the time and attention of two parents instead of one. They have more financial stability with two parents.

Having a dad just brings more security to kids in general, especially a dad who is committed to their mom and their family. They feel secure knowing that we as parents don't talk about separating or see that as an option. Divorce is not a word in our vocabulary. Father God is our example. Our Heavenly Father (Abba Daddy) makes a difference.

LOVE BECAUSE OF AND IN SPITE OF DIFFERENCES

Fifteen years ago, we brought our son into our home with only three days' notice. He was three and a half months old, and we had been brokenhearted when his birth mother changed her mind about placing him for adoption when he was born. I had always heard that parenting came naturally—that we would just instinctively know what to do. We found that to be true. He was happy and content with us from the very beginning. It was as if God had ordained it—which we are certain He did!

One thing adoptive parents have to contend with is that they are raising a child whose personality and traits are not inherited from either of them. We, his parents, are practical, punctual, and hardworking people. Our son, on the other hand, is creative and imaginative, with no concept of time. These differences can cause conflicts at times. Teenagers sometimes chafe against rules that are meant for their safety and well-being, but which they see as restrictive and unnecessary. This is nothing new. Parents have dealt with this problem since the beginning of time.

The thing that I remember most about our first meeting with our son's birth mother is that she looked my husband right in the eye and said, "I want him to have a strong father because I didn't. I don't want him to get away with anything." Even at her young age, she realized that her baby needed a mother and a father. Fathers are vitally important in a child's life. In most cases, fathers are the rule givers and the disciplinarians. Even though he is only fifteen, our son understands that we are trying to teach him to be a godly, moral, and responsible citizen of this world. He may not like the consequence that sometimes comes with the rule-breaking, but we always precede the "grounding" with why he is being punished—that we want him to learn to be responsible.

Our son is now and has always been a great source of joy for us. He is told practically every day how much he is loved and that we cannot imagine our life without him. Even though he is so completely different from us, we wouldn't change one thing about him. God gave him his quirky personality and his imaginative spirit, so who are we to try to improve on God's handiwork?

Clayton in our family has taught us that different personalities and temperaments have broadened our perceptions of others. We as Mom and Dad have made efforts and strides to really get to know Clayton deeply. We're trying to teach him to know us deeply as well. The result has been we've all learned to love unconditionally because of the differences as well as in spite of them. Mom and Dad as well as Clayton have all grown positively in these last fifteen years.

DAD'S WORDS

One of these dads stated a simple message that all the dads emphasized in his own way. Being a dad is definitely a privilege. If more men took their task of being a dad from his Heavenly Father's example, he would see it as the privilege it is.

The "calling" from God to be more than a man (a sperm donor) but a hands-on dad—an involved dad with his training from his Heavenly Father God—they'd see it as the adventurous privilege it is. The joy of the Lord will be their strength. The fine line between happiness and joy will become more visible. Life isn't all happiness. There are mountains and valleys. However, there can be joy in the midst of it all when men get their training from God, the Father, Jesus, the God example in the flesh, and the continuous comfort and counsel of the Holy Spirit in the midst of the highs and lows. That joy will override the negatives and highlight the positive highs.

Each dad emphasizes the positives of their fatherhood. Partnering has some negatives along the way. However, these dads found when they began to recall positives, those great memories far outweighed the negatives. These dads found that Father God—the perfect teacher, organizer, designer, creator, example, and more—would be with them to excitedly do it again, given the opportunity.

UNEXPECTED LIFE LESSONS

How do you prepare for a miracle? How do you learn to set your watch to God's provident timing? In our fifth year of marriage, for years we had been vigilantly praying. We had consulted medical professionals, satisfied the state requirements to adopt a child, and truly hoped God would grace us with a child. On our sixth anniversary, we enjoyed a wonderful trip to the beach. As we talked over sunsets and prayed together about what the future would hold, we found a peace imparted upon us by the Holy Spirit that we were going to be okay, and that together with Him, our life would be complete. At the time, I think we believed the feeling was that our life would be complete, even if the Lord chose not to bless us with a child. Now, looking back, I know the feeling of peace and comfort was imparted upon us by the Holy Spirit to enable us to remain calm and develop a sense of preparedness for what He had already designed and planned. While we were on that same trip, our miracle, our joy, our gift from God entered this world. His timing is divine.

We were prepared spiritually, emotionally, financially, and even personally to welcome our child, even before we knew he was on his way. From the day we learned of the wonderful blessing that is our child, to the day we thankfully brought him home, was only ten days. Not much time! It was such a whirlwind, filled with rejoicing, excitement, anticipation, some impatience, rearranging, and more prayer for what was in store. Watching his beautiful mommy wrap him in her arms the first time was beyond extraordinary. To be able to see him, hold him, smell him, listen to the funny sounds he would make, watch him sleep, and just enjoy his amazing personality, which was evident even from his first days, was a tremendous gift that was artfully and skillfully designed by an amazing Heavenly Father.

In reality, it is probably likely that we were not as prepared as we thought we were. It is true we were ready, we had the resources, and we had the support. But can anyone really be prepared to hold a tiny wholly dependent newborn in hand and be completely confident you will be able to love him, nurture him, teach him, guide him, protect him, and provide for the totality of his needs?

Our son was a little infant, less than six pounds. He had a big personality though. He seemed to have more skin than he needed and was full of wrinkles. But he was, and still is, gorgeous. Sometimes I think about the pride we have in our son, how much we adore him, and it makes me think of our Heavenly Father. When God looked from heaven upon Jesus, He declared that "this is my son, and I am well pleased." Looking at our son, it is very humbling to try to grasp the Father's love for my child and for all of us, knowing the sacrifice that was made for us.

Thinking about that increased the pressure and feeling of responsibility parenting such a precious gift from God.

It is also very humbling to attempt to articulate the ways in which we feel our son's life is more positive because we are his mommy and daddy. There is not a doubt that we, his mommy and daddy, are truly the ones whose lives are more positive because he is our son. We are the lucky ones!

I do know that my life is enriched, my faith has further developed, my relationship with Christ has grown deeper, and that I am a better man because of my relationship and marriage to my wife. At times I marvel at her grace, I admire her strength and steadfast faith, I seek her forgiveness, I try to emulate how lovingly she worships, and I am grateful that God chose her as my helpmate and wife. With that, I know I am a better parent because she is my wife. We obviously have different strengths and weaknesses. We generally fill different roles in our son's life. But filling different roles is not done to the exclusion of one another or in the absence of one another. There are days and times he wants or needs more of his mommy, and there are days and times he wants or needs more of his daddy. There are projects and experiences that he cherishes doing with both of us as well. Our family, all three of us, try to be very intentional in spending time together. I say all three of us because our son is as diligent as we are to ensure that we spend that time as a family. I am sure that will change somewhat as he grows older, but the time we have spent, and will continue to spend, lays a foundation that will serve us into his adult years.

Prior to his birth, when it came to parenting, we were jointly committed that our son (or daughter as the case may have been) would grow up in a home with parents who loved and followed God. We strive to place Christ in the center of our marriage, and in that, He remains the center of our home and our family. There will come a time in our son's life when he will leave our home and make his way into the world. As his parents, that reality becomes scarier and scarier. He will, however, have a foundation, an exposure to God, His teaching and His scripture, an understanding of His identity, and prayerfully, a strong relationship with the Lord. Our son will always be our son, and we will always love him, we will always fight for him, champion him, encourage him, and even, when necessary, chasten him and correct him. But as is the way it was intended, there will be a day when he will be responsible for himself and ultimately his family and his children. He will find a wife, a vocation, a calling beyond the safe confines of our home. He will carry with him, though, memories, lessons, examples, teachings, devotionals, prayer times, and an understanding of what a man of God, a husband, a father, and a disciple to the nations is supposed to be. He will further carry with him memories, examples, and an appreciation for and understanding of a Christ-led mother and wife. Not because his mommy and daddy have always gotten it right, or have never failed, or have never fallen, but because of the introduction our child received and continues to receive to our amazing Heavenly father; to His son, our savior and Lord; and to our comforter and counselor, the Holy Spirit.

ROLE MODEL FOR PARENTING

We will never forget when we received "the call" from Loving Alternative about being chosen to be the adoptive parents for Kenzie. While the ensuing three and a half weeks of adoption red tape was challenging, all faded to gray when Kenzie arrived! Her birth mother placed Kenzie into our arms two days later and let us leave with her! Wow, the beginning of an awesome journey.

Kenzie is ten years old now, and what a great ride it has been so far! At times, we still can't believe we get to parent her—such a joy and overwhelming blessing. Each time we reflect, the affirmation of God's perfect plan has been strengthened. God brought Kenzie to us on purpose as an answer to one simple prayer. We all wanted the provision of a "better life," but the other common thread in our case was the desire for a sibling. They wanted Kenzie to have a big brother, and we wanted Luke to have a little sister. Praise God for what *He* has done!

Reflecting on the last ten years, there are many highlights that remind us about how important it is to have both a mommy and a daddy, and an active daddy at that. Below are a few meaningful highlights we thought about together with Kenzie's help.

Love Bond. The moment Kenzie was placed into Daddy's arms, the bond has been there. Kenzie is close with both Mommy and Daddy, and David has been present and active in her life all along the way. There has not been too many a night when Daddy wasn't present to help read or sing or rock or tuck her in, pray and love on Kenzie when she goes to bed. Both Mommy and Daddy did/do this regularly, so Kenzie formed (and has) a bond with each parent separately. She experiences the difference in that bond and is familiar with and trusts those differences (Mommy vs. Daddy).

Masculine Influence. There has always been a manly influence in

Kenzie's life. Daddy's presence gives her a sense of safety and security that both resembles and differs from the presence of Mommy.

Appropriate Affection. Bear hugs, tickle battles, and snuggling with Mommy or Daddy while watching movies or before bedtime. Kenzie loves watching videos and mystery movies with Mommy and reality TV (mostly *Survivor*) with Daddy. When Kenzie just wants to rest and not necessarily watch or do anything, her go-to cuddle buddy is Daddy, who helps her feel safe and secure in a different way than Mommy does.

Activities. Hiking, biking, and playing together, or going to get ice cream or a fancy coffee…all favorite activities shared by Kenzie and Daddy. Kenzie has an adventurous and outgoing, risk-taking spirit and loves people, like Mommy and Daddy. Daddy is likely the greater influence on being adventurous and risk-taking.

Security and Safety. Feeling safe and secure as Daddy leads the family— learning how to lead and shine for God in all things (through reading His word, prayer, trying things, and encouragement). This is a regular thing (we're not perfect or always consistent), and over time, Kenzie has gravitated more and more toward engagement vs. disinterest or rebellion.

Special Occasions. Date nights with Daddy to learn how a girl should be cherished and loved.

Salvation in Jesus Christ. Baptizing Kenzie after she accepted Jesus as her personal savior in early 2019. That was a huge highlight and blessing to get to do so (Daddy).

AN ONLY CHILD

Nathaniel is a great son. Having a mom and dad has been a great positive in his life. Sometimes it may be taken for granted since that is the only thing he knows. He has a dad who worked from home his entire life. A dad who saw him every morning and prayed with him every night. A mom who loves him unconditionally and looks for every opportunity to provide a positive learning experience that will enrich his life. When he wanted to play more than communicate clearly through speech, Robin looked for ways our tax dollars could help our son. We had a speech therapist from Lewisville Independent School District (LISD) to come to our home and work with Nathaniel. He improved dramatically and went on to preschool.

Years ago I had experience in track and football at Texas Tech and wanted to get him involved in sports. I remember taking him to play indoor soccer, but that didn't resonate with him. At seven years old, he tried summer track. I did not agree with the training style he was receiving and talked with the coaches. The next year they asked me to assist by joining their coaching staff. I accepted and coached Nathaniel in the 400 and 800 meters. These were trying times. The challenge was separating Dad and coach. He had me all day and now in the evenings.

Telling him what to do was hard for him. He has so much talent, and I wanted to help him understand that he has a God-given gift. He must cultivate and develop those gifts.

That year he made it to Amateur Athletic Union (AAU) Nationals in Houston, Texas, in the 800m and ran a 2:53. That was quite awesome. To increase his exposure to situations and circumstances that would benefit him as he grows to adulthood, Robin and I took Nathaniel out of his current elementary school and enrolled him in a school that had dual language teaching. The kids learned Spanish and English. Nathaniel began his new journey in this new environment and made friends easily. Currently, he can speak and read Spanish very well.

When Nathaniel was asked what are the positives that he remembered, he said, "When I say I can't do something, my mom and dad say I can. They encourage me to have a positive attitude and to trust." We also taught him to serve others.

Nathaniel went with us to church where we were Elders and over the outreach program. It was awesome to witness him wanting to knock on doors and inviting residents in the apartments to the church event called Street Reach. He saw Robin and me knock on the door. A voice would say, "Who is it?" Nathaniel would say, "Street Reach! Street Reach!" Our hearts just swelled with joy as we looked at each other and smiled.

Our little boy fell in love with trains, especially Thomas. His interest in trains started another phase. His mom decorated his room with Thomas the Train comforters and pictures and even the big train set. As a family, when Thomas came to Grapevine, we all went. Nathaniel was so excited; this was a big deal. We rode on the train, and wow, that was a great day. Another great train experience was his first forty-five-minute ride on a Dart train to the Mavericks game.

Having both parents enabled us to have special moments with Nathaniel. For instance, I took him shooting arrows at an archery range. Another highlight was going to the NBA D-League Texas Legends basketball games together and eating chicken strips.

We spend time imparting in him who he is in Jesus and that he is special. We have core values for our home that are reflected by how he acts, speaks, behaves, and responds to situations.

We know it was God's purpose for Nathaniel to be our son. We are very grateful that his birth mom gave us the privilege to be his dad and mom. There are so many experiences we wouldn't have had or will not have if we hadn't adopted Nathaniel. We can't imagine our lives without him. He has brought such joy to us and our family. It's exciting to be used by God to help Nathaniel discover his purpose and destiny. We know God has something special for him to do. We're asking God to help us to build strong foundations of faith and love for God so he can be the great young man we know he is. When he was young, we would take our special walks. Now we're going on bike rides. We all enjoy watching cooking shows.

He's in middle school now and learning to play the trumpet. He wants to play football next year for the school. He has a gentle and loving spirit, and he brings joy to all who meet him. He's very laidback and loves life. If we said he didn't have to go to school, he'd be very happy. He just wants to have fun. He still enjoys spending time with us. We have our movie and game nights. Of course, he is not the perfect child, and we're not perfect parents, but we are perfect for each other. God put our family together.

God makes families of all sorts. Some have several close-knit children. Others are like Nathaniel's—just Mom, Dad and Nate. In God's unique knowledge, He knows which will thrive in its particular situation.

I've known families where the children all take part in the growing and nurturing of the others. Then there are those where perhaps God knew this child would thrive and fit into God's plan for him better if he had Mom and Dad to himself.

Aren't you glad the God who created all of heaven, earth, and everything in them also created all His children? In God's wisdom, He put each child in the perfect home for that child. God knows dads do make a difference.

PARENTING STARTS AT BIRTH, BUT NEVER ENDS

Any man can be a father, but it takes someone special to be a daddy.

It's important that any child has a mother and a father, no matter the sex of the child. As a mom and a female, they show them the feminine side, and Dad as the male shows the masculine side, but together there is a balance.

My relationship with my daughter is one where I try to show her through life's day-to-day activities how to achieve her best. By also showing that Daddy can be strong when I need to, and still be gentle enough to kiss her on the cheek good night or a random hug during the day. I try to show her that she can come to me about anything, yet knows there are discipline boundaries that she has to follow for her own good. Daddy is not always the fun one or the one she wants to be around in those times of discipline, but at the same time, my relationship is one where I can sit down with her and explain why she is being disciplined while showing her it's to protect her from potential hurt now and as she grows up.

I am a parent first and a friend second, as it always should be. We have a blast together enjoying games, watching cartoons, or splashing each other in the pool. At the same time as a parent, I am guarding that she does not grow up self-centered, that she thinks of others first, and that starts by making sure she respects us as parents.

As she gets older, I want to model for her how she should be treated by future boyfriends and, ultimately, somewhere way in the future, a husband. We do this by having daddy-daughter dates, but also modeling it in front of her as how I treat her mother, my wife.

A HANDS-ON DAD

We recently learned of friends who feel God leading them to adopt and have begun the home study and application process. It brought back so many wonderful but scary memories of our first days, but also made me marvel at God's goodness as we prepare to send our adopted daughter to college as a freshman this fall. How could eighteen years have gone by so fast? First off, let me say I don't think of her really as our adopted daughter. There is no difference whether adopted or birth. She is our daughter, plain and simple.

To be honest, sometimes I forget she was adopted, she is just ours… our gift from the Lord.

Brenna excelled in high school, graduating with honors. She got a head start toward her future life journey while in high school. She received endorsements in law enforcement and art. She was chief of Keller Spirit Crew, vice president of the Criminal Justice Club, captain of her Law Enforcement II class, and a Green Card member. As she starts in the fall at Stephen F. Austin State University, she plans to major in Forestry and Wild Life Management. Needless to say, her mom and dad couldn't be more proud.

My hope is that Brenna knows the love that we have for her is unconditional and unlimited, and that through my love, she knows God the Father's love for her, and that she doesn't have to search for love and acceptance from ungodly sources. Most importantly, that she will always know God's heart for her. That she will never stray from Him and always pursue His path for her life. I also pray that at the right time, God will bring her a godly husband. Ultimately, I pray that they will have a wonderfully healthy marriage.

As we raised Brenna, we always celebrated what God did through the adoption. We wanted Brenna to know the beautiful and loving aspect of adoption where some folks so often see adoption portrayed negatively. We always have honored and affirmed the love that her birth mom has for her in making the brave decision to place. Over the years, every time the topic of Brenna's adoption came up, we turned it into a celebration. We would stop what we were doing and celebrate the beauty and love surrounding the adoption and how God made us a family. We would discuss what her birth mom did and how she wanted her to have a mother *and* a father. In that, God made us a family. I don't know how many celebrations we've had, but there have been many.

I am so proud of my girl as she has grown into a beautiful young lady. I am amazed at her wisdom and discernment, her creative gifting, and her ability to put things together. She has a love for serving. Another love she has is for animals and the outdoors. I am so thankful to see her steadfast in her faith and confident in who she is in Christ. I am in awe of God's love, grace, and mercy that He granted me the blessing to be a dad—a dad to my daughter, Brenna.

I asked Brenna, as her dad, how have I impacted her life. Her response? "You're my dad. You impacted me every waking moment of my life."

This is a vivid picture, just like our adoption into the family of God. All that was because of God's love for us. The Bible reminds us that God loved us before He knew us. God's love for us is just like this dad's love for his daughter.

SECURE WITH DAD AND MOM

My wife Pamie and I both had parents in the same household when growing up. This gave us solid role models.

Pamie has said her mother didn't always come to her functions. She seems a bit resentful about that; maybe that is why she and I never miss any of Abby's functions. We both want to be a part of her activities.

Abby has bonded with me in several ways. We try to have family time but also one-on-one time with her. We are together on road trips to baseball games, walking the dog, singing in the car, swimming, and whatever can bring us together.

Abby has bonded with her mom differently than she has bonded with me. The three of us have together times, but they also have one-on-one times as well. Girl things include shopping, getting nails done, watching movies, rides in the car, and trips to the lake.

Here are some positive experiences Abby stated about having both parents in the same home. She thinks it's great; if one parent makes her mad, she just goes to the other parent.

She stated that she has noticed a difference in her home and the homes of friends whose parents have divorced. Those kids might have more freedom. This may result in a lack of discipline and security. The parents want to do things to make the kids happy temporarily. The kids may feel they are growing up by themselves without wisdom and direction.

God intended for families to have both parents in the home. Our daughter has different experiences and discussions with me than she does with Pamie, which I think is a good thing. We both have time for her. Some of the best discussions have been when we just listen. Abby has thanked me several times for letting her talk and giving her feedback without criticizing her before the words are out of her mouth.

We let her talk about things and offer her opinion. Our family is not a dictatorship. Mom and Dad are very important to her.

Pamie and I each have unique strengths as well as weaknesses. Where she needs me to fill in places that she feels need, I can often add that needed wisdom. This is also true for me. In my weaknesses, she often adds a word or two or merely listens. The Holy Spirit completes us both where we're needed to balance each other. God formed her in another womb, but God formed her in the hearts of Pamie and me—the mom and dad who make the difference.

AS THE KIDS GROW, THE PARENTS GROW

We have two adopted children. Our son is seven, and our daughter is two-and-a-half. As we write this, we are visiting the family of our older child's birth mother in Michigan. Not only is the weather a welcome respite from the heat and humidity of the Texas summer, but we are enjoying the benefits of this extended family brought together because of our unified love for our children.

So many times as adoptive parents, we are asked to imagine how much better off our kids are "because" we adopted them. We have had people innocently say things to us like "Those kids are lucky you adopted them" or "Can you imagine what their life would be like if you had not adopted them?" But that discussion is grossly unfair because it makes unnecessary assumptions about birth parents, affixes a sort of "savior" mentality to the adoptive parents, and it neglects the trauma of separation felt by so many adopted children. I do not presume that our children's lives are "better" simply because we adopted them. We did not "save" them. That is not how we view our relationship with our children, nor is that how I want our children to view us.

Instead, we prefer to focus on how the adoption process completed our family unit. We celebrate the gift and sacrifice of the birth parents, and we grieve their loss. And we, the adoptive parents, are truly the blessed ones. We are constantly reminded of how truly blessed we are to have the opportunity to love and nurture these children. *They* made us parents. *They* created our family. Not the other way around. Every adoption story is different and unique. We know that our adoption experiences are different from others.

Our two children have helped create a new world of extended family. We have a very close relationship with our son's birth family.

We did not know them before he was born. Since then, they have become our extended family. We do not have that same relationship with our daughter's birth family, although we hope to one day make that connection. Our new extended family has become a part of every Christmas, every birthday, and summer vacations.

Our two children have encouraged us to learn new things based on the things that interest the kids. On any given night, you can find our family dancing to any assortment of Disney tunes, or playing tea party with stuffed animals. And there is lots of singing. Very loud singing! These are moments we cherish. And these moments are important to our children.

***

Editor's Note: I supervised and observed this whole family in their home for six months prior to finalization of their second child. I saw Dad be a real "hands-on dad." He held, fed, burped, and changed the baby while Mom may have been entertaining the older brother. A mom's role is to nurture. She did that well. The dad's job is to be the priest in the home, protector, and the provider. As I watched this dad with their older child, it was then that I added another job to the dad's responsibilities. He is also the playmate.

***

Our two children have opened our eyes to social issues that were not readily relatable to us before. Before considering adoption of a different ethnicity, please take a moment to read this. We are white. Our children are not. We get the occasional side-eye at the grocery store, but the kids' smiles can change a mood really quickly. Some of our greatest joys are those supportive black women in line at the checkout who tell us that we are doing a good job with our daughter's hair. That said, we have cut out several friends due to some comments, "jokes," or offhanded remarks from otherwise good people who have opened our eyes to racial biases and prejudice. Racism still exists. We will fight for our children. It is not enough to simply not be racist. That is passive. We must be actively anti-racist. And we will be anti-racist as a family.

It is debatable whether our children's lives are truly "better" because of us. Of course, we like to think that is the case. But the word *better* has many meanings and different interpretations. But we do know that God has blessed us with two incredible children and an amazing family full of love and laughter. That fact is not debatable.

BEING DAD IS A PRIVILEGE

I've seen that children who are secure in their father's love are able to say no to all kinds of temptations. This is that the vacuum in their lives is already filled. They don't have to do things to win the approval of their friends when they can find the security, identity, and approval in their parents' love for them. Most of all, they have approval in their heavenly Father's love for them.

Before the age of five, my kids were already learning to drive by sitting on my lap as I drove. I've taught them how to camp, build a fire, secure the fire, fish, climb trees, build tunnels in sand piles, build super duper Hot Wheels race tracks, how to mow the yard, run a backhoe, and even drive a tractor.

I've always been intrigued with engines. Because my boys always wanted to be in the middle of anything I was doing, it was natural for me to pass on that interest in car engines. They learned how to rebuild engines and fix almost everything related to cars.

They are learning all sorts of "guy" things preparing them for manhood. A really vital lesson I taught them was "Never, ever hit a lady."

They learned by my example and lifestyle that Jesus loves us so much. He gave His life for us and still does every day. I've taught them that smiles and being happy are choices, and making that choice is always the best choice. Some of my boys are biological. Two are adopted. I forget which ones are which. Family is family. Another lesson is to always protect family and love everyone always.

Another useful lesson is "A good dog will be your friend in spite of you." We are chosen by God. Very valuable lessons come with life as we live it. They'll always be forgiven because they are all children of God. Jesus's time on the cross tells us that He forgave *all* our sins—past, present, and future. Knowing this helps us to make more sinless choices.

God uses dads to help grow families. But the ultimate finished work is from the Spirit through dads.

WE ACCENTUATE THE POSITIVE

The paradigm I had regarding adoption was that maybe a couple of high school kids were too young to raise a child. Regardless of your thoughts concerning adoption, when you become a dad, it will change you; it will change you for the better. The moment my daughters were placed in my arms by their birth mothers, my worldview changed. The love I immediately felt for my daughters was profound. I was not prepared for that. I think that is as close as I come to understanding just a fraction of the love God has for us.

When my girls were little and I tucked them into bed, I always asked them one question: "Do you know how much your daddy loves you?" They would answer, "So much!" When the girls told Mama they loved her, she would always say, "I love you more." All the girls have silver heart charms on their bracelets. On one side is engraved "I Love You More," and on the other is engraved "So Much."

We had more daddy-daughter dates than we can count. Ice cream was the favorite when they were little. One daughter loved to shop, so we would often go shopping. Mom would sometimes think we would come back with the strangest things. The answer to the question "Why did you buy that?" was always the same: "Because that's what they wanted." I would just give them a little money or price range and tell them they could have anything they wanted within that price range. They still have them. My younger daughter was just happy to be together and often told me I didn't have to buy her anything. We might just sit on the back deck, cracking peanuts in the shell, and eat till we were full. She called them crunchy peanuts. Once she discovered her love of music, we spent lots of time in Guitar Center.

Her love of art took us many times to Hobby Lobby. Anytime I went to the hardware store, I would ask them if they would like to go with me. When they were toddlers, I didn't want them to be bored, so I would ask them if they would help me by carrying something for me. My favorite thing to give them was little pieces of PVC pipe because it was small enough for them to carry easily. When they inevitably would drop one, it would bounce all over the place. They were so afraid they would get into trouble, but I would just laugh and tell them to go get it. One time I went to buy a wheelbarrow and put my younger one in the wheelbarrow and wheeled her all over the store. (In retrospect, I should have thought that through because she asked me to do that again almost every time we went back there for a long while.)

At home they often wanted to help. If I was painting, then I would put water in a coffee can, give them a brush, and tell them they could paint the porch. They had lots of fun with that.

My wife and I frequently gave our adoption testimony at events, and the girls always accompanied us. When they saw Mom and Dad on stage, they would find an opportunity to leave their sitters and come up on stage with us.

They didn't see us as speakers; they saw Mom and Dad and knew that was where they were supposed to be. One Father's Day, I was asked to give the sermon at our church. The girls were only three and four at the time, and they sat in the front row with Mom. As I spoke, the girls only saw their dad. Unprompted, they decided they wanted to be with their dad, so they got up and stood beside me the whole time. What a joy to speak about a father's love and the Father's love with the cutest girls ever by your side.

My older daughter developed a love for school and could not miss or be late. She would get upset with me about promptness. One time we decided to take a day trip to San Antonio because they were learning about the Alamo and to spend the rest of the day shopping. We worked it out in advance with their teachers but did not tell the girls. On the way to school, my older girl noticed I did not drive in the right direction. She got upset. I said, "What if we skip school and go to San Antonio for the day?" She looked me straight in the eye and said, "Dad, you better not be joking with me." They learned early that I was a jokester.

I built a playhouse with a Dutch door and a deck that matched the deck on our house. Mom would bring their lunch to them every day. They would take all their Barbie dolls and stuffed animals out there and have school. Once my younger was sitting with the dolls and stuffed animals while my older was at the podium. When Mom asked what they were doing, they said they were "having church."

We love to go camping. I love to fish, so I taught them how to cast a rod and reel. They were only about five and six. I have pictures of their first fish caught on a princess fishing pole. We would always fish a little when we would go to the Fatherheart picnics. I remember the father of a young boy asking me how I taught the girls to cast so well. My younger daughter can make a campfire without needing a fire starter while my older prefers to stay inside and read. One of my fondest memories is of my little girl coming down the steps of the RV, her arms barely able to carry the peanut butter, crackers, and milk. She was so tiny. I used to eat that when I was little, and she loved them too. Mom packed them special, so we shared them at the picnic table. They asked Mom and me what our favorite things to eat were when we were little, so we had fun making our favorite dinners from childhood. Turns out they are not as fond of beans and weenies as I was. But when I showed them how to make popcorn the old-fashioned way outside on a gas burner, they were amazed. I couldn't make enough!

We went to a daddy-daughter dance, and my older daughter told me it was the happiest day of her life! Granted she was only nine, but I was the proudest daddy there! I had donuts-with-daddy with my younger girl, and let me tell you, there were some questionable donuts that some dads had to eat.

We've taken family road trips in an RV all over the country. We've been to the Rocky Mountains, Niagara Falls, and the white beaches of Florida. The girls finally had to lay down the law and told us they were too old to go to any more museums on our vacations. To have them sitting there while we drove through the mountains for the first time in their lives is a favorite memory. Another is during one of the fifteen-hour-long days of driving, and they asked us to tell them what music Mom and Dad listened to when we were in school. We pulled up all the bands we could think of for hours.

When the girls were getting older and somewhat interested in sports, I couldn't wait. That is until they chose my least favorite sport—basketball. Why couldn't they play softball? After a few seasons, I dipped my toe into coaching as an assistant for my younger daughter's team. Trying to corral preteen girls into some semblance of organized practice is harder than herding cats. We still laugh because they only won one game the entire season. The best part is that was the only game I was head coach. Our head coach was away on vacation, so it was only me. Somehow we won, and my daughter remembers that I have bragging rights over the only win.

They moved on to volleyball. Since they were homeschooled, the league would ask a parent from each team to call lines. I think there was one season that I called lines for every game. We would drop my older daughter off for practice early in the morning. Then my younger and I would go get a breakfast biscuit till her practice time started. One time we went to Chick-fil-A to get french fries, and it was so busy they asked for a name. They didn't ask for "my" name, so I made up a name. My daughter was a little mortified at the time, but I have since seen her provide some quite clever names to the barista at other restaurants. It was also fun teaching them to pay for themselves at checkouts. We often held the line up while they counted out some change.

My younger daughter became daddy's girl and my little shadow. She has learned everything, from how to change the oil in a car to how to grill the perfect burger. I still have the old truck that I bought the same year we adopted our first daughter. The radio was not digital, so you could still hear static when you changed the station. I explained to her how it worked. Fast-forward to middle school science class. They were learning about circuits. The teacher laid out parts for the kids to build things. Mostly just circuits plugged together to light a light bulb. But the teacher threw other parts out that they could experiment with, even though they may not know what the parts were. One of the parts was a radio tuner. The other kids thought it was a speaker. My daughter recognized the sound it made and built a radio. The teacher was impressed! She knew circuits, radios, propane, transformers, all kinds of stuff. The teacher asked her, "How do you know all this stuff?" Her answer was simple: "My dad."

As they got older, they gravitated more to Mom as I was just no help with some things. Then came driving lessons, and I was back in the game. Somehow I was a calmer passenger than Mom, but it was more likely that I could hide it better. I couldn't call our outings daddy-daughter dates anymore. Ice cream took second place. It became a white chocolate mocha with an occasional extra shot of espresso or double chocolate chip Frappuccino with white mocha sauce, chocolate shavings, and a drizzle of light whip. Heaven forbid I should tell them they picked up someone else's drink order because they would provide random girls' names to the barista.

Out of the blue, my older daughter decided to get a job. A job? You just got your license! Time for more fatherly advice. Always do more than you're asked. Look for things to do, and keep busy. Do the jobs no one else wants to do and do them well. Always treat people with respect, etc., etc. She said, "Dad, I still remember the advice you gave me when I first started school. Don't worry about others. There will always be someone smarter, someone prettier, or someone who catches more breaks. Just be you. Be the best you can be." Wow, they actually listened.

Then came boys. I told them there would be no car pulling in the driveway, honking while she ran out the door yelling, "Bye!" The young man had to ask permission first and then would need to always come to the door. There was one young man with good character who asked for my permission. To hear my girls tell it, it was rather comical. He stood at least a few inches taller than me, making me look up, while I, in my best fatherly stature, asked what his intentions were toward my daughter.

I don't mean for this to sound like the ideal life. It wasn't always rainbows and sprinkles. The girls always knew they were adopted, and we helped them understand that they were loved, not just by us but their birth moms and birth families too. Their caseworkers are still thought of as family. We've had heartaches, arguments, rolling of eyes, and slamming of doors just like all families. But we choose to remember the good. We lived life.

When we filled out our adoption paperwork all those years ago, we said we just wanted to be a mom and a dad and to experience life through the eyes of a child. We wanted our children to love the Lord with all their heart and soul and mind (Deut. 6:5), be well rounded, and contribute to society in a positive way using the gifts the Lord gave them.

Life happened, time flew by, and now, they are both in college. One is on her way to becoming a doctor of pathology while the other is pursuing her calling in Christian ministry.

When our girls were placed in my arms, we all prayed blessings over them. I can say that our prayers and our girls' birth mothers' prayers have been answered. Our birth mothers chose to place their girls in a loving home with both a mom and a dad. Our daughters were raised with unconditional love, and they have blossomed into the most beautiful women of grace. They have beautiful spirits, personalities, and demeanors. They are not just sisters but are the best of friends.

Adoption made us a family. Adoption gave these girls a better understanding of life's choices. It has changed us all…for the better.

If you were to meet these girls today, you'd be amazed. They are socially mature and comfortable in any situation or group they might find themselves. It is very evident that an "involved dad" in the lives of daughters does make a difference—for good.

APPENDIX

LEGACY OF AN ADOPTED CHILD

Once there were two women
Who never knew each other
One you do not remember
The other you call mother

Two different lives
shaped to make yours one
One became your guiding star
The other became your sun,

The first gave you Life and
The second taught you to live in it
The first gave you a need for love
And the second was there to give it.

One gave you a nationality
The other gave you a name
One gave you the seed of talent
The other gave you an aim.

One gave you emotions
The other calmed your fears
One saw your first sweet smile
The other dried your tears,

One gave you up,
It was all that she could do.
The other prayed for a child,
And God led her straight to you,

And now you ask me through your tears,
The age old question through the years;
Heredity or Environment, which are you a product of?
Neither my darling, neither

<u>Just two different kinds of Love.</u>

Anonymous
Lee Ezell Ministries, Box 2983, Laguna Hills, CA 92654

"ABBA"

Paul writes, "We have received the spirit of adoption…by which we cry out 'Abba! Father'" (Romans 8:15). Adoptive parent understand these words. They know what it means to have an emptiness in their hearts, to hunt, set out on a mission, take responsibility for a child with a spotted past and a dubious future. And that's what God did for you! Knowing full well the trouble you'd be and the price He'd pay. He sought you, found you, paid an awesome price, signed the papers, gave you His name, took you home and gave you the right to call Him "Abba," which literally means, "My Daddy." Don't you love it? Adoption is not something you earn. It is all you receive. Can you imagine prospective parents saying, "We'd like to adopt little Johnnie, but first we want to know does he have a house, money for tuition, a ride to school in the mornings, and clothe to wear every day? No agency would stand for such talk. They'd say, "Wait a minute, you don't adopt little Johnnie because of what he has, you adopt him because of what he needs. He needs a home."

Paul didn't say we've earned the spirit of adoption. He said we've received it. Why's that important? Because if we can't earn it by our stellar efforts, we can't lose it through our poor performance. How reassuring! Why does any parent want a child? To love and to share their life with—and that's how God feels about you today!

"ABBA, FATHER!"

> For you did not receive the spirit of bondage again to fear, but you received the Spirit of adoption by whom we cry out, "Abba, Father." The Spirit Himself bears witness with our spirit that we are children of God. —Romans 8: 15–16

I love it when I'm in Israel and I hear little children running around in playgrounds, calling out, "Abba! Abba!" and jumping into their daddies' embraces. To the Jews, Abba is the most intimate way in which you can address your father. It's a beautiful picture of the truth that through Jesus, you have received the Spirit of sonship by whom you cry out "Abba, Father." Did you notice that the Holy Spirit refused to translate the original Aramaic word "Abba" into English?

In Abba's arms, a child is most secure, protected, and loved. No enemy can pull a child out of his or her Abba's strong arms. That's the image God wants us to have when we pray to Him and call Him "Abba." Of course, you can call Him "Daddy" or "Papa," or whatever term helps you to see God as a warm, loving, and caring Father.

Unless you can see Him as your Abba Father, you will continue to have a "spirit of bondage again to fear" (Rom. 8:15), referring to the Old Testament fear of God. It's a slavish fear of judgment and punishment that brings you into bondage and makes you afraid of God. But God doesn't want you to fear Him. He wants you to have a Spirit of sonship! Too many believers are living with an orphan, fatherless spirit. If you are entangled with all kinds of fears, guilt, and worries today, what you need is a good heavenly dose of the Father's love for you!

Something amazing happens in your spirit when you see God as your Father. If my daughter, Jessica, has a nightmare, all she has to do is cry out, "Daddy!" and Daddy is there! Jessica doesn't have to pray in King James words: "O Father that liveth and inhabiteth the next room, I plead with thee to come to me at this time of peril, that thou mayest rescue me from this nightmare!" All she has to do is to cry out, "Daddy!" and I'm there.

Similarly, in your moments of weakness you don't have to approach God with perfect prayers. You just cry out, "Daddy!" and your heavenly Father runs to you! You are not coming before a judge. You are coming before your Father, your Daddy God, who embraces and loves you just the way you are.

Take time to come to your Abba Father today. Believe that He loves you unconditionally today. See Him welcoming you with a smile on His face and with outstretched arms. Run into His embrace, bask in His perfect love for you, and let it melt away very worry, fear, and insecurity. When you believe and receive your Father's love for you, it will put unshakeable peace and strength in your heart!

THE CRY OF A FATHER'S HEART FROM GENESIS TO REVELATION… FATHER'S LOVE LETTER

My Child…

You may not know me,
But I know everything about you…Psalm 139:1
I know when you sit down and when you rise up…Psalm 139:2
I am familiar with all your ways…Psalm 139:3
Even the very hairs on your head are numbered…Matthew 10:29–31
For you were made in my image…Genesis 1:27
In me you live and move and have your being…Acts 17:28
For you are my offspring…Acts 17:28
I knew you even before you were conceived…Jeremiah 1:4–5
I chose you when I planned creation…Ephesians 1:11–12
You were not a mistake…Psalm 139:15–16
For all your days are written in my book…Psalms 139:15–16
I determined the exact time of your birth and where you would live…

    Acts 17:26
You are fearfully and wonderfully made…Psalm 139:14
I knit you together in your mother's womb…Psalm 139:13
And brought you forth on the day you were born…Psalm 71:6
I have been misrepresented by those who don't know me…John 8:41–44
I am not distant and angry, but am the complete expression of love…

    1 John 4:16
And it is my desire to lavish my love on you…1 John 3:1
Simply because you are my child and I am your father…1 John 3:1
I offer you more than your earthly father ever could…Matthew 7:11
For I am the perfect Father…Matthew 5:48
Every good gift that you receive comes from my hand…James 1:17
For I am your provider and I meet all your needs…Matthew 6:31–33
My plan for your future has always been filled with hope…Jeremiah 29:11
Because I love you with an everlasting love…Jeremiah 31:3
My thoughts toward you are countless as the sand on the seashore…
    Psalm 139:17–18
And I rejoice over you with singing…Zephaniah 3:17
I will never stop doing good to you…Jeremiah 32:40
For you are my treasured possession…Exodus 19:5
I desire to establish you with all my heart and soul…Jeremiah 32:41
And I want to show you great and marvelous things…Jeremiah 33:3
If you seek me with all your heart…Psalm 37:4
For it is I who gave you those desires…Philippians 2:13
I am able to do more for you than you could possibly imagine…
    Ephesians 3:20
For I am your greatest encourager…2 Thessalonians 2:16–17
I am also your Father who comforts you in all your troubles…2
    Corinthians 1:3–4
When you are broken hearted, I am close to you…Psalm 34:18
As a shepherd carries a lamb, I have carried you close to my heart…
    Isaiah 40:11
One day I will wipe away every tear from your eyes…Revelation 21:3–4
And I'll take away all the pain you have suffered on this earth…
    Revelation 21:4
I am your Father and I love you even as I love my son, Jesus…
    John 17:23
For in Jesus my love for you is revealed…John 17:26
He is the exact representation of my being…Hebrews 1:3

And He came to demonstrate that I am for you, not against you…
Romans 8:31

And to tell you I am not counting your sins…2 Corinthians 5:18–19

Jesus died so that you and I could be reconciled…2 Corinthians 5:18–19

His death was the ultimate expression of my love for you…1 john 4:10

I gave up everything I loved that I might gain your love…Romans 8:32

If you receive the gift of my son Jesus, you receive me…1 John 2:23

And nothing will ever separate you from my love again…Romans 8:38–39

Come home and I'll throw the biggest party heaven has ever seen…
Luke 15:7

I have always been your Father and will always be Father…
Ephesians 3:14–15

My question is…Will you be my child?…John 1:12–13

I am waiting for you…Luke 15:11–32

…Love, Your Dad
Almighty God

www.ingramcontent.com/pod-product-compliance
Lightning Source LLC
LaVergne TN
LVHW040157080526
838202LV00042B/3205